THE TRUMP CARD

A Psychiatrist Analyzes Reactions to Donald Trump

Colin A. Ross, M.D.

Manitou Communications, Inc.

1701 Gateway, Suite 349
Richardson, TX 75080
Phone: 1-800-572-9588, FAX: 972-918-9069

www.rossinst.com
www.manitoucommunications.com
rossinst@rossinst.com

Library of Congress Catalog Number: 2017906008

Ross, Colin A.

The Trump Card: A Psychiatrist Analyzes Reactions to
Donald Trump

ISBN: 978-0-9986601-1-0

1. Donald Trump 2. American Politics 3. Political Satire

ALSO BY THE AUTHOR

TABLE OF CONTENTS

INTRODUCTION: HELLO RUBY TUESDAY

Pleased to meet you
Hope you guess my name
But what's puzzling you
Is the nature of my game
I stuck around St. Petersburg
When I saw it was a time for a change
Killed the czar and his ministers
 Anastasia screamed in vain

Sympathy for the Devil, The Rolling Stones

By the way, in England, if you tease, satirize or make fun of someone, it's called "taking the Mick" out of the person. That's what I am going to do in the subsequent pages of this treatise. I hope you don't find my words too jagged, you on the left, or you on the right. I turn it to the left, and I turn it to the right, then I turn it all around. That's what it's all about!

I'm not apolitical, but this is a political satire.

THE RORSCHACH CARD

When I was a resident in psychiatry, I was taught about the Rorschach Ink Blot Test, which was invented by a Swiss psychologist, Hermann Rorschach, near the end of the Dark Ages. My very psychoanalytical supervisor explained to me that the Rorschach is a projective test, and is used to find out what is going on in a person's subconscious mind. You can't just ask the person because, by definition, we aren't conscious of our subconscious minds. The only exception to this rule is if you ask someone inside a submarine because there the sub conscious mind is conscious so the person knows what is going on in his or her sub conscious mind.

The Rorschach consists of a series of cards. The person is shown them one at a time and asked what they see in the card. Several of the cards look like bats or butterflies. If you say that these cards look like a bat or a butterfly, then the psychologist administering the Rorschach knows that you are normal. Unfortunately, he also knows that you are boring.

If you are shown one of the bat-or-butterfly cards and answer, "That looks like Donald Trump saving America," then the psychologist knows that you are a Republican.

On the other hand, if you answer, "That looks like Donald Trump destroying America," then the psychologist knows that you are a Democrat.

Neither of these responses is rational. Both are reactions of the unconscious mind. In gastroenterology, such reactions are called belching. They are treated with medication. On American cable TV news channels, such reactions are called political commentary. They are reinforced with lots of airtime and, if you are lucky, some really big, really beautiful salaries.

Scenario number three: if you answer, "That looks like a man hacking up his mother's genitalia with an axe," then the psychologist knows that you need psychoanalysis. Or, it could just be normal locker room talk.

In this treatise, I am adding another card to the Rorschach deck: a picture of Donald Trump. I am then going to analyze reactions to Donald Trump by sundry citizens of the United States of America. Just as in an actual Rorschach Ink Blot Test, I am going to analyze what these various - not nefarious - citizens project onto the Trump Card. Since I am a psychiatrist, this means that my analysis of reactions to the Trump Card is objective, scientific and professional. There is no way that I am projecting the contents of my subconscious mind onto the projections of the citizenry's subconscious minds onto the Trump Card. That would be way too confusing. And unprofessional.

"Harrumph! I say, Basil, is this treatise ever going to begin?"

"It already has, Cecil, it already has."

"Quite right, Basil, quite right! Carry on, then!"

THE POLITICAL PERSPECTIVE OF THIS HERE DOCTOR

As you may have gathered from the Introduction to the present treatise, I have Sympathy for the Devil. But the devil is in the details. So think of this as a devil detail, a military operation to infiltrate the subconscious minds of the citizenry.

In the interests of full disclosure, I thought I should make my own political affiliation clear, for the record, in case there is ever an audio version of this book. I don't have any political affiliation.

Is that clear enough?

This is an equal opportunity book. You have the right to be targeted with satirical jokes whether you are on the left or the right. I don't discriminate on the basis of race, gender, culture, religion, or political affiliation.

Actually, if you really harassed me on it, I would probably say something lame like, "I'm socially liberal but politically conservative."

The problem is, in the current climate, this response would get me hated by the extreme right as a bleeding heart liberal, and hated by the extreme left as a white middle class male chauvinist pig. The extreme left never hates female working class African Americans, because they do discriminate on the basis of gender, race and social class. Similarly, the old fart white guys in the Republican party would never get caught in a seedy motel with an under-age male African-American prostitute, only a white one.

THE IQ OF AMERICA HASN'T CHANGED

In therapy sessions, I sometimes have to educate the person I am working with on the IQ distribution in different races, cultures and civilizations. This can be somewhat difficult for them to understand, because they don't live in a civilization. From a cultural perspective, they live in a post-apocalyptic wasteland, one as barbaric as the landscape inhabited by Mad Max. They don't realize that this is so because the apocalypse is hidden behind an array of technological devices and material wealth – but they nevertheless do live in a world without memory or history.

In our present-day cultural wasteland there is no living history. Any love of history, any feeling for history as a real, living thing, part of one's own personal life, is gone, dead, deceased. I remember when I was living in England, spending many hours over at my French girlfriend's house – Patou Lardillier – God rest her soul. I never met her father but her mother and step-father were good, solid working-class people. He was English and owned a small bar, so he technically was not exactly working class. But working class they were.

I remember going grocery shopping with Patou's mother one day – a short walk in the neighborhood. We stopped at the butcher's, then the bakery, one small shop at a time. She knew the people in each shop and chatted with them in a friendly, warm manner. We got one or two items here, one or two items there. It was a different world. I grew up in Winnipeg, Canada eating plastic Wonder Bread and plastic Kraft cheese slices. It is amazing how lousy the cheese and bread were in Winnipeg.

But more amazing – just because she wanted to, because that is what she enjoyed, Patou's mother used to read the French classics in her spare time. This humble working class woman was more educated, more truly educated, than anyone I had ever met in Canada in the fifties and sixties. She actually lived in a real culture. Her daughter ended up frying her mind with LSD and other drugs, but I have always remembered that grocery shopping expedition.

Here in Amerika we have late night comedians on TV. They often have segments in which a person goes out on the street in LA and asks random people on the street questions. For example:

"If you drove south from here, what is the first country you would enter?"

Response: "I don't know."

"In what year was George Washington President of the United States?"

Response: "Uh. . . 1954?"

"What is the name of the ocean near here?"

Response: "The Atlantic Ocean?"

"What is the capital city of France?"

Response: "England?"

Yet, these scholars can immediately crank out the correct answers to countless questions about pop music and movie stars. It isn't a problem with IQ. History, geography, literature. These subjects are dead to them, killed off by the educational system. Sure, they memorized enough boring historical facts to get a high school diploma, but the educational system made them hate history and literature. Nice job, Professors of Education.

This is the problem in Amerika the Beautiful. The complete failure of liberal arts education. The dumbing down of America till it has become a caricature of itself. Picture the stereotypical American tourist of the nineties, socks halfway up the calves, sandals, shorts, a Hawaiian shirt, and a camera slung over the shoulder. Speaking not a single word of any language other than English, and not much English. It's an embarrassment.

The reason that the IQ distribution comes up is that the person I am working with (who is filled with self-blame, self-hatred and suicidal ideation) has just explained to me how stupid she is because she has only a high school education. To correct this "cognitive error" – the psycho-lingo in use these days – I explain that in fact, the distribution of IQs is the same everywhere in the world. There are just as many people with IQs of 140 per capita in the Amazon jungle as there are in Dallas. Of course, the denizens of the Amazon jungle would bomb out on a standard IQ test, but this is because western IQ tests can't measure their intelligence.

Finishing high school, or college, I explain, doesn't change your IQ. I don't get into the failure of liberal arts education, because my goal is to focus on the person I am working with, and to help her lift some of the burden off her shoulders – the burden of bad self-image, low self-worth and high self-blame and self-hatred arising from severe, chronic, complex childhood trauma.

As I quip in one of my aphorisms published in Adenocarcinoma and Other Poems: "There are many ignorant professors."

I've met many professors who have fancy degrees and can talk fancy boring academic talk, who are very ignorant human beings. Petty, back-stabbing, small-minded, obsessed with academic politics, etc., etc. I've also met some really brilliant professors who I admired greatly. But, from a cultural perspective, we live in a post-apocalyptic desert. This doesn't mean that we are lacking in eggheads. It just means that most people in America have no living sense of history. History is in boring books. It isn't something you feel in your heart and gut.

It's kind of like asking the average NFL football fan about opera – boring, boring. For the average NFL football fan, opera is "culture." Listening to some music professor intone about the aesthetic complexity of The Barber of Seville results in no detectable EEG response in the football fan. Little does the football fan realize that football is living culture in America. It is inconceivable to most Americans that anyone could have the same feeling about "culture" that football fans have about football, trucks, tailgate parties, beer and hot dogs. Inconceivable.

Normally, talking like this gets you pigeon holed as a snob. A cultural elitist. An intellectual. Maybe even a serial killer or a sex offender. Something really bad. And, too often, the intellectual elite is a bunch of disconnected eggheads. The eggheads think the boors are boors and the boors think the eggheads are eggheads. The foibles of each party reinforce the attitudes of the other party. Both parties are correct and both are missing the point. It's not that football and culture are two separate categories. Football is culture. I'm a football fan. I say that football games are really enjoyable cultural events.

Culture doesn't have to mean boring, dusty, dead, intellectual monotony. It can mean an amazing post-catch yardage statistic. But notice the way it works: boors versus eggheads. The boors call themselves real people and they are right. But their culture has been eroded for over a century, their popular culture. In the meantime, the culture of the intelligentsia has eroded at the same pace. The whole shebang is sick.

Did I say boors versus intellectuals? Sorry. I meant Republicans versus Democrats. The Trump Lovers versus the Trump Haters. Fortunately, we have God on our side, according to both sides. The two sides use different terminology, but self-righteousness reigns supreme on both sides. Welcome to America. The same disease affects the entire industrial world.

WHAT I'D TELL TRUMP IF I WAS HIS ADVISOR

If I was appointed to be Trump's advisor, it would be a good day for pigs, since they would no longer have to walk, and would have the luxury of flying to work. Also, Satan would be happy to get some relief from the heat. So it would be a big day. For ease of edification of the nation, if you please, for ease of edification of the nation, if you don't please, I will, henceforth and furthermore, not, repeat not, refrain from subdividing said recommendation of the first part, the second part and possible additional parts into subdivisions, which is possible due to MDs now qualifying to be Secretary of Housing, based on extensive experience knocking on doors, not to mention knocking up nurses. This has nothing to do with treating psychosis. But it will be my mother's fault if I move to New Zealand. Henceforth, being of sound mind, I would advise 45 as follows:

RECOMMENDATIONS CONCERNING BEHAVIOR AND STYLE

1.   Tweets

Donald, enough with the tweets, already! Really, I'm serious. I realize they are part of what got you elected, but really. . . do we have to begin the campaign for 2020 right now? Just because the Democrats have already started? I realize you have 20/20 vision and can see things very clearly, but really? And reacting to what Hollywood actresses and pop singers are saying has got to stop. Meryl Streep is over-rated as an actress? Come on. Don't let Madonna get your goat, you old goat. Stay cool. Be cool. Be Presidential.

2.   Over the Top Statements

Again, I realize that your behavior got you elected, so who am I to suggest you change your style? Also, I get it that some of your absurd statements are actually opening positions in a negotiation process and I get your success at the Art of the Deal, but nevertheless, do you have to be so extreme? So often? If the goal is to win over some of the centrist undecided, maybe the strategy could use a tweak. On the other hand, if the strategy is to stoke up the polarization, enrage the bleeding heart liberals and thereby provoke a right wing counter-reaction to liberal extremism, resulting in your sucking the undecided centrists towards you in the ensuing vortex, I get that. Good move, Lao Tzu! Or do I give you too much credit?

3.   That Billy Bush Thing

You would think that a Billy Bush locker room talk tape would sink a candidate, but then we have to remember that Bill Clinton's ratings went up after the Monica Lewinsky scandal.

Maybe the voters thought, "Good for you, you old dog!"

Maybe the voters were secretly scornful of wife Hillary. Maybe playing that card in the Presidential debates was a smart move. It sure stung Bill, as you could see from the expression on his face, sitting there beside his loyal daughter while you debated his loyal wife. Hillary versus Melania – not a close race. Maybe you should tone it down in the Oval Office – but then again, raunching it up worked for Bill's popularity ratings. I guess the only conclusion we can come to is that voters are a little conflicted about male-female relationships. I have a feeling Hillary wouldn't have done well on The Apprentice. I bet you would have fired her ass for not being hot enough. Oh yeah! Wink, wink, nudge, nudge. High five, man! God bless the Locker Room! Chicks dig it! Well, maybe not chicks but at least rural Caucasian voters seem to, but then they're always digging things out there on the farm, so digging locker room talk is second nature for them.

And don't worry about Bill. He gets it. Just give him a good back slap at the Trilateral Commission and everything will be OK. Or the Bilderburger World Hamburger Championship, or that island in the Caribbean where Bill flew on that private jet, wherever works for you. The boys get it. And the First Ladies and other female members of the Club get it. Boys will be boys! Reminds me of the incest moms who know what's going on but throw their daughters under the bus in order to keep their incomes and public images at the PTA. Very understandable. What else is a girl going to do? What? Set limits? Impose boundaries? Consequences? Divorce? Integrity? What? No way.

You know, funny thing is, maybe Hillary could have beaten you if she'd divorced Bill after Monica and Jennifer and whatever those couple of dozen other women were named. Maybe her behavior was the opposite of her supposed liberal feminist values, and standing up for women and children and God Bless America! (or at least the half that votes Democrat). But what did she do? She stood by her man. This is exactly what the extreme right wing evangelical Christian Bible thumping horrible Republican wives wanted her to do – it's right there in the Bible! Maybe Hillary's left wing feminist base secretly despised her for standing by her man. But then they couldn't come out and say that because maybe they needed Bill to campaign for Hillary and thereby swing the undecided voters who aren't sure if it's cool for a married man to get blowjobs from a 19-year old intern in the Oval Office. Good thing she wasn't 16!

Boy, talk about sexual politics!

4.   The War on Drugs

Mr. President. You're a businessman. You know how things work. The War on Drugs is going nowhere. We have three approaches to drugs and alcohol in America: 1) a military/paramilitary model where we nuke the suppliers 2) a medical model where we treat the consumers for their disease 3) a psychological model where we use the Twelve Steps or rehab or psychotherapy. None of these models are getting the job done. I say that as someone who treats addictions with psychotherapy, and I think my work is helpful, but it's just a drop in an ocean of addiction. Not enough people are truly motivated to do the arduous, painful, complicated work of recovery.

I advise you to change the model. Look at the drug problem in America as a business problem. Put together a black budget and send some people down to meet with the cartel bosses. Make stopping the drugs from coming into America more profitable for them than selling the drugs. And make them responsible for shutting off the supply chain. I leave the details up to you – you're the creative businessman.

But in case you're having a senior moment, here's an idea. Evaluate the cartels' annual gross revenue: X billion per year. Then come up with a figure for their overhead. Then offer them net + 10% if they shut off the flow of cocaine and heroin into Canada, Mexico and the US. Production has to stop – it can't be diverted to other countries. I'm asking you to do this for Canada as a favor and for Mexico as a favor to them and to set up a virtual wall between the US and Mexico. Don't worry about low-level dealers – just get the snake to cut off its own head. But have lots of free methadone on hand for free withdrawal and detox beforehand. Maybe throw Europe into the deal, or whatever countries you choose, maybe the whole world.

This will piss off some people making a lot of money off of prisons, drug enforcement and legal fees, but ask me if I care. Divert the resources to snuffing out the meth labs inside the US. If you do this and the liberals find out they will hate you but what they don't know can't hurt them. Maybe the cartels would like to invest in some hotels instead.

5.   The War on Terror

The War on Terror is righteous and it sure sells lots of guns and ammo and Toyota trucks, which is great for business. Again, I'd look at it as a business problem. Just buy all the guns that are being sold to the terrorists, on the condition that the flow to the terrorists has to stop. Deal directly with the manufacturers. Islamic terrorism isn't a clash of civilizations – it's a business problem. Use your business mind. Your business mind can actually get things done. The way to disarm the terrorists is to cut off the supply of arms. I realize this still leaves machetes, but you can't fix everything. Anyway, I think the US military can deal with machetes.

You know, Mr. President, you're off on the body count. As we know, the seven countries you put on the immigration ban have resulted in zero deaths from terrorism on US soil. Sure, sure, some bad guys have been foiled. All the evidence is classified, but I'll take it on faith. Let's look at the body count in the twenty-first century, using the best available guesstimates:

Gun suicides (17 x 18,000)	306,000
Gun homicides (17 x 14,000)	238,000
Child Abuse and Neglect (17 x 1,400)	23,800
Domestic Violence (17 x 1,300)	22,100
9/11	2,977

The war on children and women waged by terroristic husbands and fathers (including a lot of Republicans and Democrats) has killed a lot more people in the twenty-first century than died on 9/11. And the 9/11 death toll is dwarfed by the gun murders and suicides. How about if we devote federal resources in proportion to the body counts? I know, I know. The contractors making money off the War on terror will be upset, but they're big boys. They can diversify.

6.   Strategic Defense Initiative

Mr. President, if you're ever attacked by a mob of clowns, go for the juggler.

7.   Don't Call the Hombres Hombres

In my professional opinion, Senor El Presidente, you come across as a nerd trying to sound like a bad ass when you refer to Mexican criminals as bad hombres. I realize you want to be seen as a bad hombre yourself but it just makes you seem like a clown. Plus it's outrageously inflammatory. Maybe a tiny tiny but really beautiful touch of diplomacy might be a consideration.

Again, however, I can't really argue with success. Amazingly, your bombastic reality TV style and outrageous over-the-top comments got you elected. Nice one. But, on the other hand, I guess it's not really amazing. The US Presidential race, from the primaries to the outcome of the election, is now officially a Reality TV Show. It operates at the level of the Housewives of Beverly Hills, or New Jersey, or Pennsylvania Avenue – doesn't matter where, it's all the same level of entertainment.

It's all about the ratings, whether it's The Apprentice or the Real Live Presidential Race Show. What does it take to get ratings? The more outrageous, the more over-the-top, the better. You played the game perfectly, it turns out. So why would you need my advice? You don't, so I'll give it for free. Maybe, just maybe, now that you're in, you could consider toning it down a bit. But you won't, I know – why? Because the race for 2020 is already up and running. You can't afford to slack off too much.

Which leaves me wondering. . . Obviously, you're an incredibly successful businessman. And obviously, this required a lot of smarts, a lot of negotiation skills, and a high level of risk tolerance. Great qualities. So here's what I can't figure out – is all this buffoon behavior just you, or is it strategy? Is there another Donald behind the reality TV mask? A President even? I don't want the first option to be true, so I keep hoping for the second. But sometimes you make it hard to hang on. Other times, you behave fine and seem balanced, diplomatic and Presidential – then, zing, out comes another doozey. Back and forth, back and forth. . . hard to know.

WHAT'S WRONG WITH TRUMP?

What's wrong with Trump? This is a trick question. The trick is, I'm not going to answer it. I've heard that Donald Trump is a narcissist, likely a psychopath. That statement is made by left wingers, Democrats and liberals. They all think Obama was the cat's pajamas. They never accused Obama of being a narcissist. Flip the mirror on the wall and what do you see? Who's the most narcissistic of them all? I was told, during the dark days of the prior administration, that Obama was a narcissist. I remember one friend of mine telling me that he had just read an article in which a "leading" psychologist reached this conclusion. Sorry to spoil the suspense, but my friend is an ardent Republican. He never said Reagan was a narcissist.

"Mirror mirror on the wall, who's the most narcissistic of them all?"

"You're the one looking in the mirror, my man."

I think that psychologists and psychiatrists making "psychological profile" comments about US Presidents is dumb, bad, wrong, unprofessional, below the standard of care and downright poopy. That's about as strongly as I can put it. It's all circular. They reach their foregone conclusion based on their political views, but pose as professional analysts making some kind of scientific analysis. Posers! Poopy posers, petunias – I'm getting perturbed pontificating about them, so I'll stop.

Well, one more thing. In psychiatry textbooks, we call this all-or-nothing, black-and-white thinking. In the chemical dependency world they call it stinking thinking. In DSM-5 it's called devaluation-idealization (you can tell psychiatrists are really smart because they use big words). In DSM-5, this extreme black-and-white thinking is a diagnostic criterion for borderline personality disorder – it's a symptom of mental illness. Such thinking has become the norm in our culture, whether it's polarized debates about abortion, immigration, gay rights, or raising or lowering taxes. It's a war of sound bites, the more outrageous the better!

I'm not psychoanalyzing Donald Trump because he's not the patient. He's a symptom. The patient is our culture.

The question is not, "What's wrong with Donald Trump?"

The question is, "What's wrong with our culture?"

Analyze That.

WHAT WAS TRUE THROUGHOUT THE CLINTON, BUSH AND OBAMA ADMINISTRATIONS?

Here is a short list of things that have been true throughout the Clinton, Bush and Obama administrations, and will still be true after the Trump administration, in all likelihood. We could call this list The Dirty Dozen. The United States:

1. Has over 40,000 gun murders and suicides per year compared to dozens or hundreds per year in other countries in the industrial world.
2. Has 5% of the world's population and consumes 80% of the world's prescription narcotics.
3. Has a higher incarceration rate than any other country in the world.
4. Ranks in the 20's-30's-even 40s on numerous world indices including physical health, happiness, infant mortality, and educational outcomes in high school.
5. Spends more per capita on health care than any other country but has lousy outcomes.
6. Spends more on its military than the next ten countries combined.
7. Is the only country in the industrial world where people go bankrupt because of cancer.
8. Has the most polarized, vicious, partisan politics of any country in the western world.
9. Is the only country in the western world not to sign various environmental treaties.
10. Is the only country to have used atomic weapons in war.
11. Is the only country in the western world with as many guns as people.
12. Has the highest rate of obesity of any country in the western world.

Anybody want to debate whether or not the body politic is ill? There were dire predictions that Obama was going to destroy America. He was going to establish a Communist state, destroy the economy with socialism, appoint himself to a third term, and then become a dictator. Did it work out that way? Not quite. Were there reasons to be concerned about Obama's tendencies in that direction? How about the fact that two of his senior advisors were documented domestic terrorists?

Hold on! What? Conspiracy theory! Conspiracy theory! Right wing propaganda!

Maybe not. Maybe that's just a fact. Maybe Bill Ayers and Bernadette Dorn were members of the Weather Underground. Maybe. Maybe. Not sure.

"I say, Basil, no need for sleepless nights. Take your medication. Everything will be quite all right. Stay chipper, old chap!"

"Thank you, Cecil. Thank you. I feel better now."

"Sleepy time, Basil, sleepy time. The opiate of the masses is a great medication! You can count on it"

The fact of the matter is that Barack Obama did not destroy America. Nor did he save it. He ran up the national debt by $10 trillion smackeroos and change, however. That's more than the net worth of one hundred billionaires, so I don't think you can pay that off by taxing the top 1%. Think it's good for the people to run up that kind of debt? Maybe not, maybe not.

The fact of the matter is that Donald Trump is not going to destroy America. For one thing, US Presidents don't really have that much power and control. It's nice to feel safe because a Good Father in the White House is taking care of everything and keeping you safe. It's really scary when a Bad Father is in there. I mean weally weally scawey for liddle kids. Weally weally.

During the Obama administration, I was concerned about America tipping over into a right wing fascist state. Now I'm concerned about it tipping over into a left wing fascist state. Checks and balances, checks and balances, but where's the balance?

Note: due to reticence, social appropriateness, and insufficient fact checking the author has not mentioned that the United States of America is one of the countries that still has the death penalty. The exalted list of death penalty countries includes:

- Afghanistan
- Antigua and Barbuda
- Bahamas
- Bahrain
- Bangladesh
- Barbados
- Belarus
- Belize
- Botswana
- Chad
- China (People's Republic)
- Comoros
- Congo (Democratic Republic)
- Cuba
- Dominica
- Egypt
- Equatorial Guinea
- Ethiopia
- Gambia
- Guatemala
- Guinea
- Guyana
- India
- Indonesia
- Iran
- Iraq
- Jamaica
- Japan
- Jordan
- Kuwait
- Lebanon
- Lesotho
- Libya
- Malaysia
- Nigeria
- North Korea
- Oman
- Pakistan
- Palestinian Authority
- Qatar
- St. Kitts and Nevis
- St. Lucia
- St. Vincent and the Grenadines
- Saudi Arabia
- Singapore
- Somalia
- South Sudan
- Sudan
- Syria
- Taiwan
- Thailand
- Trinidad and Tobago
- Uganda
- United Arab Emirates
- United States
- Vietnam
- Yemen
- Zimbabwe

Wait a minute! Hold on there! The list of death penalty countries includes all seven countries on the Trump immigration ban, plus a lot of other Arab Muslim countries. Oh, and North Korea. No wonder we don't want to let those barbarians in at the gates! They might start executing American citizens. Thanks for protecting America, Donald!

PROJECTION OF THE BAD SELF

Sigmund Freud was one seriously wacked out individual. His theories of penis envy and castration anxiety are sicko. He said that little girls literally, consciously want to have their fathers insert their penises in their vaginas. This is normal talk for an incarcerated pedophile. When psychiatrists talk that way, they call it the Oedipal Complex, because they're a lot smarter than pedophiles. Despite his criminal level of depravity and flagrant sexual psychopathology, Freud was actually a very smart cookie. He figured some shit out. One thing he figured out was a bunch of basic defense mechanisms, for example, displacement.

Displacement is when you are angry at your boss but you don't want to get fired so you go home and kick your dog (or your wife, if you're a Republican). You displace your anger from its real target onto a substitute, safer target. This is a really smart strategy, unless your wife is one of those women who likes to cut penises off, which could be true of Republican wives, which could be why their husbands are so uptight and hostile.

Another Freudian defense mechanism is sublimation. This is when you transform an unconscious or slightly conscious conflict into something higher and healthier like a work of art, instead of acting out the conflict. So, if you're a Republican and you feel like raping your neighbor's wife, instead of doing that, you could sublimate your impulse. For example, you could write a Grammy-winning rap song about bitches and ho's. Throw in some guns and a tricked-out ride, and some flash shoes, and you've got a healthy work of art instead of a crime. Hmmm, well, maybe not exactly – maybe that's not a good example. Anyway, sixteen in the clip and one in the hole.

This Freudian shit is hard to swallow, I mean semen, I mean theory – sorry, Freudian slip there. I'm no coprophiliac! Look that one up, sucker!

Yet another Freudian defense mechanism is projection. This is where you have some feeling or impulse but you're very conflicted and uncomfortable about it. You could try denial, or sublimation, but there's another option – projection. This is where you feel angry and hateful so you project your anger and hate onto someone else. Then you're a good boy or girl because you're not angwy at all. You holy. You saint. Not like those angwy, angwy, bad, bad Repubicans. Whoops, another one of those pesky slips slipped out. Did I say Repubicans? They're always focused on the pubic interest, we know that. They sure have some penetrating insights; you'd almost think they're psychiatrists. Sixteen in the clip and one in the hole.

But enough of the Freudian negligees.

There is a ton of projection going on in the United States of America. It's a big theme in reality TV and in politics – oh, whoops again – I forgot – they're the same thing.

Oh, and one other thing, before I forget that. . . there is another Freudian defense mechanism called reaction formation. Reaction formation is when you take on the opposite feelings and behavior from what you really feel and want to do, as a defense against those feelings. For example, guys who go out and beat up gay men are actually very uncomfortable about their own homosexuality, so they cover it up with big boots, big trucks, big belt buckles and big Bibles.

Another example of reaction formation is the public persona of Hillary Clinton. I remember watching her interview on Zach Galafinacky's Between Two Ferns. I was quite astounded when Zach told her that she was dressed "like a librarian from outer space." Pretty ballsy by the Zachster! But what do you think is under the lid of the prim and proper business lady Hillary Clinton who really cares about the women and the children and the people? Appearances are not what they seem. Imagine if Hillary went to the Oscars in one of her typical outfits. She wouldn't fit in very well in Boobywood. Her outfits are actually a signal – men want the non-threatening librarian in the White House, not the babe. Hot babes sometimes swing both ways and they might seduce your wife, which wouldn't be hard to do given the competition the average late middle-age Caucasian conservative white male provides. But no worries, Hillary is safe.

It's completely contradictory. The crusading feminist in the ordained-by-the-patriarchy outfit! The champion of women wearing the outfit prescribed for her by the white male conservative elite! The Boss Lady prim and proper! You wouldn't want the women on the red carpet at the Oscars showing up at church in those outfits, that's for sure. God didn't make female breasts and He sure didn't want them paraded around in the Garden of Eden, or Hollywood or anywhere. Look what happened to Lot's wife when she disobeyed. Not pretty.

Oh well, it's Washington. What else do you expect? Sex and politics. How long has that story been going on? When Hillary plays the asexual role, she's still playing a part in American sexual politics. A role prescribed for her by the corporate and political elite, not to mention the Vatican. Except the Vatican would never allow a woman to be President because they've got a better lockdown on their social system. I'm not saying there were ever underground tunnels connecting medieval monasteries and nunneries, because that's just a conspiracy theory. Holy sons of God molesting the sons of their church members – do you think there might be some reaction formation going on in those randy celibate servants of God?

Back to projection. Let's say you have a self-image of being a very inclusive, tolerant, liberal person but you have a nasty streak you don't want to admit is lurking inside you, because that wouldn't fit with your Mr. Nice Guy (or Ms. Nice Gal) self-image, wouldn't meet the expectations of your equally liberal and tolerant friends, and might make your mother be disappointed if she found out about it. What can you do? You could try to stuff it. Basic denial is always a good strategy. But what if that darn gosh heck angry mean streak just won't stay suppressed? You could get drunk, but then the lid really comes off and watch out friends and neighbors!

A back-up strategy is projection. Disown it at all costs – project the mean streak out onto someone else so that it's in them. Gone! Poof! Solved! Now, you are a very tolerant, liberal, inclusive person, not like those bigoted Republicans and their racist, xenophobic, misogynist, top 1% President – he's not my President! See the beauty of projection. Everything you condemn in yourself is no longer in you – it's all out there, projected onto the enemy. Beautiful.

There are several problems with the defense strategy of projection. First, it means that whenever you are criticizing the opposition, you are actually telling the world about yourself. The intolerance in our culture currently includes not just homophobic white supremacists, but liberal intolerance of the right wing. This is what the liberal sees in his or her mirror. Mirror, mirror on the wall, who's the most intolerant of them all? Next problem: when you are talking about "reality" it is really all internal reality, not external reality. The world has become your personal Ink Blot Test. Mix in a tincture of deliberate government disinformation, add two ounces of paranoid conspiracy theory, and it's impossible to tell what news is real, what is opinion, what is projection. . . you're not in Kansas anymore!

Speaking of conspiracy theory, it is a fact that Big Brother is watching. The evidence? If I search for hotels in a certain location or flights to a certain location, what shows up in my Facebook within 24 hours? Ads for hotels in that location and flights to that location. My search has been monitored, logged, analyzed, fed to a chain of third parties and then exploited for potential profit. So, what sounds like a paranoid conspiracy theory is just a fact. Inversely, what sounds like a fact can be someone's projection onto the facts. That's a fact. Or no, that's my opinion about the facts, so it's a fact that that is my opinion, we just don't know if my opinion is factual. That's the web of fake and fact and facts about the fake we live in, for a fact.

When you project The Bad Self out onto The Opposition, then you've made it very clear that you're not one of the Bad People. This is important for your inclusive tolerant friends to know, so that you don't get excluded from the loving circle of The Good People.

Aphorism #12 from "One Hundred Aphorisms: On the Nature of the Spirit," published in my 1989 book, Adenocarcinoma and Other Poems:

"We tolerate anybody who will tolerate us." The motto of the liberal.

It's very easy to tolerate yourself and your friends whether they're black, brown, yellow, gay, straight, or trans, as long as they all hate Donald Trump. Hating

Donald Trump is righteous because God is on our side and we are Democrats and this is Our America, it doesn't belong to you farmers and people who voted for Satan.

Are you grasping the concept of projection as enunciated by Sigmund Freud?

THE PROBLEM OF ATTACHMENT TO THE PERPETRATOR

The problem of attachment to the perpetrator is one of the two fundamental components of my Trauma Model Therapy. Colin calls it that. Which reminds me of the time I called my neighbor two doors down to ask if his son could mow the grass while we were out of town. The son's first name was Ross. In order to protect the innocent, I'll use a fake news last name for him and call him Ross Tapper, which was the real name of a boy in my Junior High School in Winnipeg, Manitoba, Canada. Ross' dad answered. Here's how the conversation went:

Me, "Hi. Is Ross there?"

Ross' dad, "Who's calling?"

Me, "Colin Ross."

Ross' dad, "I know you're calling for Ross, but who's calling?"

Me, "Colin."

Ross' dad (getting annoyed), "I know you're calling for Ross, but who are you?"

Me, "I'm Colin Ross."

Ross' dad, "I know you're calling for Ross, but who are you?"

Me, "I'm your neighbor. I live two doors down. My name is Colin Ross. I want to talk to your son, Ross."

Ross' dad, "Oh, OK, just a minute."

That's not fake news. That conversation really happened.

But back to the problem of attachment to the perpetrator, which is the topic for the present moment. Back to the present, then, which from the perspective of that conversation with Ross' dad, is actually the future, because the present is the future's past. For the people I work with in psychotherapy, however, the past, present and future are all mixed together, because the unresolved trauma of the past is dominating life in the present and the future. The people I work with in psychotherapy live in the past and see the present as just more of the past, stretching into the future without relief. For them, going back to the future accomplishes nothing, because the future is just the past that hasn't happened yet.

I treat mammals, principally Homo sapiens – in the future I might branch out and treat politicians, but for now I limit my practice to Cro-Magnons. If you are a mammal, and if your goal is survival, you are confronted with a very ugly problem on your first day of life: you are totally dependent for survival on adult caretakers. You can't run off in the jungle and forage on your own, because you can't even sit up or crawl. Over eons of evolution, mammals have developed an infant survival strategy: they are biologically programmed to bond, connect, attach to, love and need to be loved by adult caretakers. This isn't a choice or an option, it happens automatically. If you don't believe in evolution because you belong to the Holy Roller Church of Republican Christian Science, then it's the same thing – God designed mammals to bond and attach to their adult caretakers.

This isn't about race, gender, IQ, culture, personality type, or any other individual characteristic. It's about being a mammal. In a healthy family, this all works out OK. Mom and dad are consistently present, they love you unconditionally, nothing bad happens and you form secure attachments.

If you grow up in a big trauma family, however, it's a very different story. In a trauma family mom and/or dad are perpetrators of physical, sexual and verbal abuse, emotional and physical neglect, and abandonment, in combinations that vary from family to family. Not to mention older brothers, uncles, grandpa, and dad's friends. Now the young mammal has a terrible problem: how to form a secure attachment to your primary caretakers when they are also your perpetrators. This is a painful, confusing problem and is way too complicated and overwhelming for any child to figure out or solve.

Two opposite motions are set up: approach and avoid; love and hate; bond and detach. When you touch a hot stove, a brain stem/spinal reflex makes you pull your finger away before you've even thought about it. This instinctive withdrawal does not require intellectual analysis by the cerebral cortex. It just happens. It's the same with psychological trauma – the child fears, flees, avoids, shuts down and does whatever it can to escape the painful stimulus. Problem is, the perpetrator is also the person you depend on for survival. You can't run away into the jungle because you'll die if you try to survive on your own.

The ultimate survival imperative is, at all costs you must attach. You have to create the illusion, from the perspective of your attachments systems, that mom and dad are OK and safe. To do this, you can't afford to see, know and feel the whole picture. You have to break your psyche apart into two channels (not literally, metaphorically). I call these Mode A and Mode B. Mode A is approach, bond, connect, love and attach. Mode B is fear, hate, avoid, shut down and disconnect.

Some people with unresolved trauma get stuck in Mode A on a long-term basis. They become passive, dependent – codependent – and don't express any anger ever. Other people get stuck in Mode B – they are chronically angry, they push people away, and they don't need nobody for nothin'. Others bounce back and forth from Mode A to Mode B in a chaotic fashion, depending on what is going on in their environment and how people are treating them.

The motto of people who bounce back and forth from Mode A to Mode B is, "I hate you, don't leave me."

In psychiatry, this is called the borderline dance. People with borderline personality disorder usually get treated pretty badly by the mental health field. They are regarded as manipulative nuisances who do destructive things for no good reason. I was taught by mechanisms of primitive social conformity, reinforced by the threat of ostracism, to look down on borderlines, who were all female, from a disdainful, chauvinistic height. I was given permission to speak about them behind their backs in a condescending, dismissive, belittling fashion. This is what I was taught by my learned psychiatry Professors.

People with borderline personality disorder can indeed be manipulative, stressful to deal with, and deceitful. Those survival skills were taught, modeled and reinforced by their parents, over and over and over. But what does this have to do with the Trump Card and projections onto it by the populace?

A great deal of "political discourse" in our cultural is actually just mouthing off, insulting people, and trying to prove you're more righteous than people who disagree with you. It's the same Mode A, Mode B pattern that characterizes borderline personality disorder. Our whole culture is borderline. There's the Good Mom and the Bad Mom, the Good Dad and the Bad Dad. Although the borderline's parents were often abusive, absent or neglectful, they were also present and OK some of the time. With rare exceptions, such as Adolph Hitler, the archetypal purely evil figure, no one is all bad. There's some good in everyone.

The survivor of severe, chronic, childhood abuse and neglect often comes to treatment idealizing the Good Mom and hating Bad Dad. Indeed, this pattern of alternating idealization and devaluation is a diagnostic criterion for borderline personality disorder in the Bible, I mean the DSM-5. There are plenty of reasons to hate Bad Dad, but the underlying problem is often the opposite: it is too painful to love Good Dad and too painful to hate Bad Mom. The solution is black-and-white thinking: Mom is all good and Dad is all bad. That way you don't have to feel the pain and conflict of the underlying ambivalent feelings.

In therapy, often, the task is to feel, acknowledge, express and learn how to handle the buried opposite feelings: I love the Bad Dad who hurt me and I hate the Good Mom who failed to protect me. It's complicated, painful work, and it takes a long time. But it can be done. I have seen it done, many times.

Trump is the Bad Dad for the extreme left and Obama was the Bad Dad for the extreme right. Everything is clear and simple, the teams wear different-colored jerseys, and the game goes on. You might say that this book, The Trump Card, provides a psychoanalysis of our culture. There is an awful lot of anger, violence and acting out in the USA. A lot of murders, a lot of drive-by shootings, a lot of angry, polarized partisan politics. I wonder where it all comes from? Childhood trauma, maybe? The anger, black-and-white thinking and idealization-devaluation get acted out, reinforced and sanctioned by the supposed leaders of our culture – the politicians – who squabble day in and day out in a destructive, infantile fashion.

THE LOCUS OF CONTROL SHIFT

The other main pillar of The House that Ross Built, aka, Trauma Model Therapy, is the locus of control shift. I know, I know, it sounds Biblical, which will please the evangelical Christian right, but it's not. The locus of control shift is not about plague, pestilence or locusts. There is no t at the end of locus. If there was, then the entire theory would just be right wing locust-pocus, or hokey-pocus, or maybe even honkey-pocus, and next thing you know we would bring back segregation. No, this is the locus of control shift.

I came up with the term, locus of control shift, after listening to hundreds of patients in my Trauma Programs, who are 90% women, 10% men – why only 10% men, you might ask? In my professional opinion, it's because men are too scared to feel their feelings and do the hard work of recovery. The weaker sex is actually stronger in that regard. What did I hear these survivors of severe childhood abuse inside their families say, over and over and over again?

"It was my fault. I was bad. I caused the abuse. I deserved it."

These statements were preposterous. No child causes or deserves abuse. The self-blame of the patients created a puzzle, which I puzzled about, since I like solving psychological puzzles: why were so many otherwise intelligent people, mostly women, endorsing such a preposterous belief? It clearly had nothing to do with their IQs. Of course, they were inpatients in psychiatric hospitals, so you might expect some disturbed psychology, but not only were the people I was working with endorsing high, high levels of self-blame, they were also holding onto the self-blame very tight. Why, I asked myself?

I had to think about this puzzle a lot for a number of years before I figured it out. This is why I coined the term locus of control shift. I realized that this self-blame is normal childhood thinking, persisting into adulthood. How do children think – all children, regardless of race, culture, gender, IQ or personality style? They think the way children do – I am at the center of the world, everything revolves around me, and I have this magical power to make things happen. This is the mind of the magical child. It is Piaget and developmental psychology.

There is a very big, very beautiful literature on developmental psychology. It's an entire sub-field within psychology, with courses, textbooks and zillions of research papers and experiments. For example, young children in what is called the sensory-motor stage of development or concrete operations, do not think like adults. They do not understand the conservation of volume. If you take a bunch of three or four-year olds and do a demonstration for them, they all know what is going on.

The demonstration is: you have a tall, thin glass beaker full of water; you pour the water into a wider, shorter glass beaker, without spilling a drop. Then you ask the kids which beaker had more water in it. They all know the correct answer is, the tall beaker. This is obvious, because the column of water was taller before the teacher poured it into the shorter beaker.

If you repeat the experiment with ten-year olds, they also all get the correct answer: it's the same amount of water, it's just in a different-shaped beaker after the pouring. These children understand the conservation of volume. The IQs of the two groups of kids are the same – it's not about IQ. It's just how kids think. As they get older, kids gradually learn to think more like adults, which is a big problem in our culture, given how the adults think and behave.

When it comes to personal relationships, and family behaviors, all little kids think the same way: I'm at the center of the world, everything revolves around me, and I cause everything that happens in my world. Fortunately, most children come supplied with a female domestic service unit called Mom, whose sole function is to take care of them. Some have to make do with a sorry male substitute unit.

Let's imagine there is a fairly healthy family somewhere, say in Texas. Everything is OK, there is no abuse or big trauma. The four-year old girl in the family is doing well. Then, all of a sudden, dad moves out. Clearly, this wasn't in fact all of a sudden, but as far as she can tell it was. What is true for that girl on that day? Her future just crashed, and she feels abandoned, sad, powerless, helpless and trapped. These are the normal feelings that match the reality of her situation.

But here we are, well into the twenty-first century. This annoying little girl has her own IPad, plays games on her mother's IPhone and has already done six Power Point presentations at her pre-school. And, as if that wasn't enough, she has signed up to do a PhD in Sociology at a remote learning institution, one that does not discriminate on the basis of age, gender, race or religion.

This little girl emails off to her Professor, "Professor, I've finished gathering my field data for my thesis!"

The kindly Professor emails back, "What are your data? Send them to me."

The girl responds, "My data are, Daddy doesn't live here anymore."

The Professor replies, "Nice work. I like your sampling methodology, and your literature review was very thorough, but to get a PhD you have to have a theory to explain your data."

"Oh," says the girl to herself, "I forgot about the theory part."

She spends some time researching the matter, and finally she gets it: "Daddy doesn't live here anymore because I didn't keep my bedroom tidy."

This is a very dumb theory. It is completely out of touch with reality. What's wrong with this little girl? What psych med does she need? There's nothing wrong with her, except that she's sad and feels helpless and powerless to bring her dad back. This little girl has shifted the locus of control, from inside the grownups, where it really belongs, to inside herself. She caused Daddy to move out because she didn't keep her bedroom tidy.

This is a little four-year old sociologist using normal childhood thought processes and vocabulary to explain to herself what is going on in her world. The locus of control shift happens automatically because this is how kids' brains work. It isn't an option. It just happens.

Once the locus of control shift sinks in, a light bulb goes on: "I'm not powerless, helpless and trapped. I know what the problem is. It's me. I'll tidy up my bedroom, Daddy will see I'm being a good girl, he'll forgive me, he'll move back in, and everything will be OK."

The locus of control shift happens automatically, and it carries with it an illusion of power, control and mastery. I know what the problem is, I've got it contained inside me, and I know how to fix it. It's purely an illusion, but it protects and buffers the child from feeling sad, trapped, powerless and hopeless. Therefore the child holds onto it very tight. This is good, except for the price tag attached to the illusion of power, control and mastery: the badness of the self. If I'm the cause of bad things happening to me, then I am bad, but that's good because then I can fix things.

Check back in thirty years. Maybe everything has worked out, maybe not. For the people who come to my Trauma Programs, everything hasn't work out. Most of the time, they are depressed, suicidal, and full of self-blame and self-hatred. The locus of control shift is alive and well and dominating life in the present, because past, present and future are all the same thing. These are survivors of severe, chronic, complex trauma inside their families. I never feel happy when I hear politicians rhapsodizing about family values. For many children in America, family values mean sexual abuse and emotional neglect.

The self-blame and self-hatred get reinforced over and over and over as the person grows up, by the abusive uncle, the abusive, bullying schoolmates, the sexual abuse perpetrator high school coach, the date rapist in college, the first abusive husband, the second abusive husband. . . on and on it goes. The locus of control shift also gets reinforced by negative self-talk and negative, self-destructive behaviors. It's OK to cut on me because that's all I deserve. It's OK to stay in an abusive marriage because that's who I am – it's always been like this.

It's pretty hard to be in a healthy relationship with another person when you hate yourself. Also, you've learned over and over that the Good Dad or Good

Uncle soon enough turn into the perpetrator, therefore you can't risk getting close to anyone because you always end up getting hurt. So you go through life encased in a suit of psychological armor: I hate you, don't leave me. When a person comes close, you feel threatened, and when they leave you feel abandoned. It's not a fun way to live.

The locus of control shift also solves the problem of attachment to the perpetrator. It's much better to be a bad girl with good parents than a good girl with bad parents. That feels much safer. The locus of control shift is like an evil transfusion. All the bad aspects of Bad Mom and Bad Dad are shifted inside the self, where they are contained and stored. Mom and Dad have now been sanitized and are safe attachment figures, for a while, until the abuse happens again, then you realize that they are bad and scary, so you run away, physically or emotionally. But you can't run away too far for too long, because you depend on your perpetrators for your survival.

It's an endless cycle of trying to feel good about yourself but not being able to because the abuse and neglect prove how bad you are, which is good, because now you have contained the problem and can work on a solution. But the solution is an illusion – the problem never actually gets solved and the abuse goes on and on, until you get big enough to fight back or move out on your own, often into an abusive marriage at a young age. What should be good is bad and what should be bad is good.

In therapy, we work on reversing the locus of control shift. We want to get rid of the self-blame and self-hatred. You'd thinking that reaching this goal would be all good, but it isn't. It's bad, because when you stop blaming yourself, it throws you into a fundamental realization: I loved the people who hurt me, I was hurt by the people I loved. I felt both sets of feelings, it was overwhelming, I couldn't fix it, and I felt small, scared, sad, lost and lonely.

In the United States of America we solve this problem every four or eight years by taking the power back and voting out the Bad Dad and voting in the Good dad who lives in the White House and is all good, just like the good cowboys on TV westerns in the fifties who wore white hats. The bad guys were the ones in the black hats. Everything was clear back then.

We combine this voting behavior with a healthy dose of projection: I'm not bad because I'm not a Republican versus I'm not bad because I'm a Democrat. I good, you bad. I magical kid. I have the power. I feel the power. I beat you next time, in 2020, since you beat me in 2016, but I beat you in 2008. Everything was good back then.

Wait a minute, no, no ,no. That's not right. I beat you in 2000 and 2016. You just won twice so far this century, but I've won three times because God is on my side, not your side. I good because I have my Good Dad in the Big White House, not your Bad Dad. I good good good. I no feel bad underneath. I no projection onto you. Not me. I good.

GOD AND HIS EVIL SON SATAN

Where did this problem of hostile bipartisan politics in America originate? It's been around for a long time, at least since the Dark Ages. In my 1995 book, *Satanic Ritual Abuse: Principles of Treatment*, I review the history of Satan in western culture and Christianity. It turns out that the bat-winged Satan who lives in a burning Hell under the earth didn't exist in early Christianity and is only vaguely described in the Bible, in terms of his physical appearance. The archetypal image of sulfurous Satan was not created until the 13th or 14th centuries, so it's not part of the direct Word of God in the Bible. It's a European cultural creation.

Nevertheless, the problem of Good and Evil has occupied theologians for thousands of years. Some religions don't have a Satan or a Hell. Islam and Christianity do, despite the fact that they're supposed to be enemies, at least radical Islam and radical Christianity. Enemies with a shared cosmology. Huh. Funny. But not so funny. Both opposing factions march around the Middle East and Afghanistan with guns killing the Bad People. Both have God on their side, except that one team calls Him Allah. Geez, the things you have to do to sell guns these days! There's not enough money in votive candles.

Here is a conversation that actually took place between two college-educated, professional women in Texas, one a Catholic and one a Protestant:

Protestant Woman, "Catholics aren't real Christians."

Catholic Woman, 'Why?"

Protestant Woman, "Because Protestants are the original Christians. Catholics came later."

Protestant Woman hadn't stopped to consider why Protestants are called Protestants. What were they protesting against? Beats me. Maybe Catholicism. But who cares. History is so boring.

Here is another conversation that actually took place between a Protestant woman and her mother in Texas:

Mother, "The Bible is the word of God. Everything in there is exactly what Jesus said."

Daughter, "Mom, it can't be exactly what Jesus said because he didn't speak English,"

Mother, "What do you mean?"

That's how it goes in Texas. I believe the World Headquarters of the Flat Earth

Society may be in Texas. Why do I say that? Here is another Texas conversation:

Grandmother, "The earth is flat. The proof is in the Bible."

Daughter, "Where? Where does it say that?"

Grandmother, "It says in the Bible that the angel Gabriel blew his trumpet from the four corners of the earth. He couldn't do that if the earth was round."

Theologians have spent a lot of hours and pages pondering the relationship between good and evil. In Texas, this problem is easily solved: Texas football teams are good, and Oklahoma football teams are bad. But the theologians are always wrestling with the complexities. This keeps them in business for millennia, since they have created a core problem that can never be solved: the relationship between God and Satan, Good and Evil within monotheism. Here's how it works.

There is only one God. Your God is just a Fake News God. Ours is the Real News, the Good News. Praise the Lord. That's why we have a Good News Bible, so we don't have to read your stinky Fake News Bible.

The monotheistic God has three properties: he is omniscient, omnipotent and omnipresent. He is Everywhere, All Knowing, and All Powerful. He lives in a Big White House in the sky, not that one on Pennsylvania Avenue. Also, God is good and He loves all his children, except those Islam people and those non-evangelical fake Christians who read the wrong Bible and go to the wrong church, not to mention those feminist, baby-eating Wiccan pagan witches and other people like that. Oh, and homosexuals.

But God is good and He is everywhere. He built Heaven and Hell and created the Garden of Eden and Adam and Eve and all the animals and plants and everything. Everything. He also created Satan, who is Evil. Satan was so bad that he got kicked out of Heaven. God gave him his own place to live called Hell. If you are bad and don't obey God he might turn you into a pillar of salt or send you to Hell for a really long, long time, so watch it. God would only do that because He loves you, just like He loves Satan but had to show him some tough love for his bad behavior, like pride and stuff.

Wait a minute! God is Good. God is everywhere. Satan is Evil. God created Satan and Evil because He is good, which was a very good thing to do. That way He can test your faith and send you to his own personal Guantanamo Bay if you are bad, where you will get some really serious enhanced interrogations. In God We Trust. That's why we built our own Hell for terrorists, over there in Cuba, a country ruled by an evil Communist dictator, who's probably in Hell himself now.

As soon as you create a God who is omnipotent, omniscient and omnipresent and All Good, but also populate the universe with an Evil Satan, you have a problem. Several problems. Why would a Good God create Evil? But more troubling, if God is everywhere and in everything, that means He is in Satan, and Satan is made out of God, because everything in the universe is God. So that means God is Evil, or has a pretty big evil streak inside Him. But that can't be true because God is Good. Allah isn't good because he isn't really God and doesn't deserve a capital H in his pronoun.

Once you set up this problem, you have to engage in endless mental gymnastics to resolve it, which you never can. But you sure can write about it for centuries, while telling the masses what to do and how much tithing they owe because they aren't smart enough to be theologians. When a church taxes you, it's called tithing – when the government tithes you, it's called taxing. Some Christians in Texas sure are proud of how much they contribute in tithings every year, because this proves how much they earn, which proves how wonderful and good they are, not like those lazy welfare recipients. When Christians render unto the church what is Caesar's this is called Christian charity and tithing.

The battle between Good and Evil goes on inside God. All the players in the battle are parts of God and parts of God's plan. God gave Job boils because He loved him so much, and He sent the Egyptians plagues because He hated them so much, but He's not Evil because He's Good. He just hated Sodom and Gomorrah and also homosexuals who gomorrahize each other all the time.

The religious and psychological foundation of our culture is an endless war between Good and Evil, fought by opposing team members who are actually all God's creations and parts of God. But they sure don't act that way. None of this has anything to do with American politics. I don't even know why I brought it up. Must be some kind of gastroenterological problem I have.

I remember reading Milton's Paradise Lost. It's kind of tedious and kind of interesting at the same time. It's not the Word of God, it's the word of John Milton. It is a dramatic work of fiction, written as poetry. Fiction. Made up by John Milton. Not the Word of God, the word of John Milton. In Milton's fictional story there are characters named, God, Jesus, Satan, Beelzebub and a bunch of others. Remember, these are characters created in a work of fiction written by a human being. That's why Paradise Lost is completely different from the Bible, which was written by God, not some English poet buried in Westminster Abbey along with some other losers like Gerard Manley Hopkins and T.S. Eliot.

There is one scene in Paradise Lost where Satan is getting the boys together to plot strategy. He gathers them together in an infernal huddle (somewhat similar to what Oklahoma football teams do) and whispers to them about his plan to take over the earth and rule it. He has to whisper so that God doesn't overhear and thwart his dastardly plans, which are actually part of God's plans, since He is everywhere.

This makes Satan a tragic figure. He doesn't get it that God is everywhere and sees all things for all time, due to His really high-tech National Security Agency surveillance systems, so poor old Satan can never outwit or out-fox God. He is an impotent but tragic figure, doomed to endless battles in a war he can never win.

Jesus, on the other hand, is a very different character in Paradise Lost. He spends all of his time brown-nosing to God, currying favor with Him, and carrying out His plans for Him. Jesus is like a junior executive in a corporation, trying to score points with the CEO so that he can sit at his right hand side, and maybe even be COO some day. It's like a sardonic religious satire, except that Milton saw himself as a good, devout Christian. Jesus has to run around covering for God all the time, in Paradise Lost, because the God of Paradise Lost is an erratic vengeful tyrant who can fly off the handle at any time, and order drone strikes on anyone. Or locust strikes, depending on His weapon of choice.

TRUMP AND HIS FAKE BUDDY PUTIN

Just so everybody is clear: America = God, Russia = Satan. Well, right now anyway. My father fought in World War II, for the Canadian Army, and was wounded near the small town of Laren in the Netherlands, late in the War. He had elements of PTSD for many years. I went to a lecture by F.R. Leavis, the English literary critic, in Cheltenham in the 1960's – Leavis was a stretcher-bearer in World War I. So this is living history to me, not just facts in dusty books.

In World War II, Russia was our ally in the war against Germany. We were friends. True, Stalin killed 20 million of his countrymen, but we overlooked that for the greater geopolitical good. During World War II, the equation was: America and Russia = God, Germany = Satan. Now Germany is on our side, even though Michelle Obama wasn't too happy about her husband flirting with that Merkel woman.

These alliances change every few decades or half-century or so. Take that fabulous documentary by Michael Moore, who is not a big Trump supporter. Fahrenheit 9/11. It contains a 1983 news clip in which Donald Rumsfeld is shaking hands with Saddam Hussein because they have just closed a deal for the US to arm Saddam to fight against Iran. Flash forward a couple of decades and we are invading Iraq to depose the Evil Dictator Saddam Hussein because he has weapons of mass destruction and was behind 9/11 and what about those uranium tubes! They sure posed a clear and present danger to the United States of America.

So, our buddy who we were arming to fight our Holy Jihad against Evil Iran, was transformed in two decades into the Evil Enemy. We went in, bombed the Hell out of his country, captured him and his Evil Sons and had them executed. We did this because God is on our side and we were fighting for democracy. It had nothing to do with oil.

Oh, oh, fake news problem. Saddam Hussein had no weapons of mass destruction and he had nothing to do with 9/11. But the country bought the propaganda, Congress bought the propaganda, Hillary Clinton bought the propaganda, and in we went. Technically, the word on Saddam Hussein may not have been fake news. Maybe it was the best intelligence available at the time, honestly gathered, honestly analyzed, honestly reported to the President, and honestly passed on to the UN by Colin Powell.

OK, let's go with that. If that's true, then the CIA is incompetent and we are depending for our security on a bunch of bumbling bureaucrats posing as spies. I don't buy it. I just don't buy that the CIA is that incompetent, or rushes to judgment that prematurely. It just doesn't make sense.

What really happened? Why did we invade Iraq, really? I have no idea, but I bet it was because Saddam Hussein pissed somebody off, was disobedient, and needed to be turned into a pillar of salt. Who or what he pissed off, I have no idea. Or did we really invade Iraq unnecessarily based on bad intelligence by a bumbling CIA? I don't think so.

We did the same thing with Manuel Noriega. He was a good puppet in Panama, helping keep the illegal drug economy going for us, and then all of a sudden, we invaded Panama, captured and deposed him, and put him in a US jail for life. Why? Can anyone tell me why it suddenly became necessary to invade Panama? What security threat did Noriega pose to the US? Again, there has to be a real reason, behind the fake news = propaganda.

Getting more obscure, why did we invade Grenada in 1983? The reason given: to depose a Communist dictator there. Well, fine, except that it doesn't quite make sense that we have to invade a small Caribbean island with a population of about 91,000 in order to protect the United States of America. What threat could that little island pose to us? We needed a backup justification to feed to the American populace. We had to invade Grenada to protect 600 US medical students studying there, who might have been captured and held for ransom. Might have. This was a future crime. We had to invade a sovereign nation and depose its leader because of a crime that hadn't been committed yet. I guess there was no Minority Report on that one. The pre-cogs were unanimous.

The invasion of Grenada was all Donald Trump's fault. He probably had business dealings there.

Flash forward to 2017: tune into Saturday Night Live, which provides the best political satire on American television. That shirtless Putin is hilarious, and Alec Baldwin is also hilarious as Donald Trump. Not as good as Tina Fey impersonating that woman who can see Russia from her house, but good. What's that woman's name again, the Christian family woman from Alaska whose kids are having babies out of wedlock fairly often? Hard to remember, since her and Hillary have been rotated off of Saturday Night Live and it all happened so long ago.

Sarah Palin for Vice-President? What was John McCain thinking? I wonder why Obama won?

On Saturday Night Live it's funny entertainment. When the politicians get into it on the American Politics Reality TV Show, that's another matter. How obvious is it that this whole Trump-Putin thing is Democratic propaganda? It's as obvious as the Kenyan birth certificate story about Barack Obama. Sorry Trump, the tables have been turned now that you live on Pennsylvania Avenue. But man, the ratings are good!

You can't help but admire all these talking heads on the cable TV networks who do their Trump bashing week after week after week. Good Democratic soldiers all. No fake news there. Not like on Fox News, which spreads fake news about Obama all the time. I think it shows a lot of integrity to be living off Trump while self-righteously attacking him. Real character. It's an anti-Trump industry that attracts advertisers, keeps networks afloat, and pays the bloated salaries of the commentators.

Why is it bad to try to have a cordial working relationship with Russia? I don't get it. Would we rather demonize Russia and push the nuclear clock closer to midnight? Sure, let's antagonize the Hell out of Evil Russia. That's a good way to keep America secure! Go for it! And we sure don't want any help from Russia fighting the war on terror. No siree! Let the American taxpayer foot the bill. Only a Bad Dad in the White House would have Vlad Putin for a buddy.

There is now a Washington and corporate media industry feeding off the Trump-Putin story. Trump is bad because he did business in Russia. Trump is bad because some of his people talked to Russians before the inauguration. Trump is soft on Russia. Trump doesn't care. On and on it goes. It's all a card game. The Democrats crank up the polarization of Russia versus America, then make Trump bad because he isn't hawkish enough on Putin. Who knows, if Trump goes completely off the reservation, he might even talk to Putin and try to de-escalate tensions between Russia and America, which would be very, very bad. We definitely want more tension in the world.

It's all been flipped. Good Obama was hawkish on Russia. Bad Trump is soft on Russia. But I thought it was the Republicans who were the hawkish war-mongers, like Evil George W. Bush. Now it's all reversed. Trump is bad because he is trying some diplomacy. Obama didn't fool around with that left wing shit. Or no, I'm confused, wasn't Obama left wing?

Scandal alert! The Russians have been hacking us! They do that because Russians are evil. We here in the Boy Scouts of America never hack anybody because we're the Good Cops. The most incredible thing is that the populace buys this stuff. Nobody has a bigger surveillance industry than the US. We collect everything we can from everybody. We hack into Iranian nuclear plants, although we deny it. We hack into Angela Merkel's cell phone.

FAKE NEWS: THE ELECTRIC GRID IN BURLINGTON, VERMONT

On Friday, December 30, 2016, a comet blazed across the sky of the United States of America. It electrified the nation. The real media that never reports fake news reported on the facts. To quote:

Gov. Peter Shumlin, Sen. Patrick Leahy and Rep. Peter Welch issued statements Friday night expressing concern about the incident.
Shumlin said in a statement, "Vermonters and all Americans should be both alarmed and outraged that one of the world's leading thugs, Vladimir Putin, has been attempting to hack our electric grid, which we rely upon to support our quality-of-life, economy, health, and safety."

You may never figure it out on your own, so I'll help you: Sharp Shumlin is a Democrat. Don't shun 'em – he's fighting for you and America. Same with Leahy and Welch – great Democratic patriots fighting for your safety and tax dollars. I'm not sure if there's a pattern here, but if I figure it out, I'll let you know.

Within a few days, the news that Trump's buddy, Vlad Putin (aka, Vlad the Impaler) had hacked into the Burlington, Vermont electrical grid was a tiny bit modified. Now the facts were that Vlad hadn't hacked into the grid at all – it was just one computer that wasn't connected to the electric grid. Then there was one further tiny modification of the facts: the computer wasn't hacked into by Russia at all. It was just a routine virus. Then the whole story disappeared from the Honest Abe Mainstream media, never to be mentioned again. Now the skies of America were dark and safe again. The comet never happened.

But God damn that Donald Trump is destroying America! Him and is pal, Vlad! We better report on that fact!

SOME GAY FAKE NEWS

Here is another variation on fake news, an article from the Hollywood Reporter posted on www.msn.com on March 5, in the Year of Our Lord 2017:

Russia Considers 'Beauty and the Beast' Ban Over Gay Character

Vitaly Milonov, a Russian politician and member of the United Russia party, is reportedly urging culture minister Vladimir Medinsky to screen the film to make sure it doesn't showcase elements of gay propaganda.
"As soon as we get a copy of the film with relevant paperwork for distribution, we will consider it according to the law," Medinsky told BBC.
The potential ban comes after a drive-in theater in Alabama announced it won't be screening the film because it features a gay character.
"When companies continually force their views on us we need to take a stand. We all make choices and I am making mine," the business said in a statement on Facebook. "If we can not take our 11 year old grand daughter and 8 year old grandson to see a movie we have no business watching it. If I can't sit through a movie with God or Jesus sitting by me then we have no business showing it."

This is real news but it has a fake news spin. Notice that the article wasn't entitled, "Homophobia in Alabama" – instead the focus was on Russia. It's another anti-Trump propaganda piece. The tactic is guilt by association: Trump is buddies with Putin – Putin runs Russia – Russia is homophobic – Trump is homophobic – hate Russia – hate Trump – love America – vote Democrat. But it's all deniable. We're just reporting the news here.

Oh, and guess what, Robert Bentley, the Governor of Alabama, is a Republican.

And guess what else? Here is some real news from Wikipedia:

On March 8, 2006, the Alabama State House voted 85–7 in favor of Amendment 774, a constitutional amendment to the Constitution of Alabama which bans same-sex marriage and a "union replicating marriage of or between persons of the same sex" in the state. On March 11, 2006, the Alabama State Senate approved the bill in a 30–0 vote. On June 6, 2006, Alabama voters endorsed adding the amendment to the state's constitution with 81% voting in favor.

So Amendment 774 isn't just an aberration pushed through by a small minority in Alabama – 81% of Alabamanites voted in favor of it. But the media is so preoccupied with anti-Trump propaganda that it skips over the government-mandated homophobia in the USA in order to bash Russia.

In a counter to what I am pointing out, Democrats might accuse me of conspiracy theory. Colin Ross thinks Hollywood is conspiring against Trump in a Grand Scheme coordinated by George Clooney! That would be typical. Run the counter-response up to the maximum and demonize the person you disagree with. Standard operating procedure – on both sides of the aisle. There doesn't have to be any centrally run conspiracy. Everyone knows what to do on their team. Both teams claim that God is on their side. God hates gay people versus God loves gay people.

If I'm against the Holy Republicans on gay rights, that doesn't mean I have to approve of anti-Trump propaganda tactics. Democrats should tone down the anti-Russia self-righteousness. Such tactics just perpetuate the squabbling, fake news, extremism and cultural violence that dominates "public discourse" in the Not United States of America. This is true no matter what God thinks about homosexuality.

And Man made God in his own image.

THE ABORTION DEBATE IN AMERICA

There is an abortion debate in America. One side burns their bras and marches in the streets. The other side goes to church and pounds their Bibles. Both sides are equally vociferous and self-righteous. The "debate" isn't run by the rules of an actual debate, however, because it isn't a debate, it's a shouting match. But then again, a debate and a shouting match are the same thing these days.

The abortion debate can never be resolved. Why? Because it's a matter of faith, on both sides. In terms of logical structure, both sides make an opening assumption: abortion is righteous versus abortion is sacrilegious. Everything said on both sides follows automatically from the opening assumption in a Grand Holy Tautology. You can't prove whether abortion is right or wrong because it's a matter of faith – or, in secular terms, a matter of opinion.

How do both sides handle this problem? The Republicans frame it as a religious issue and say that God is against abortion. The Democrats frame it as a secular issue and say that it's about women's rights (which are holy). If you are in favor of abortion, you are against God. If you are against abortion you are against women. On one side, God Trumps women, on the other side, women Trump God.

Notice that the bra burners don't mention anything about men's rights. Men should have no say in abortion, according to the burners. Women get to override and can kill a man's baby any time they want, while it is still a fetus. If a man tries to block an abortion, he is against women, and against a woman's right to control her own body. But the father literally has 50% "ownership" of the fetus genetically. A fetus isn't just another part of a woman's body, like her arms, legs, breasts. . . the fetus is genetically 50% the father. If a man argues this point, however, then he is treating a woman's body as property and trying to control a woman's right to control her own body. Obviously (at least it's obvious to me), a baby being conceived by rape should result in the rapist having no rights of any kind including no right to block an abortion. Also, I am not talking about a situation in which an abortion becomes a life-saving necessity for the mother; that situation is a statistical outlier. The "abortion debate" is 99+% about fetuses conceived through consensual adult sex.

For feminists to maintain their position that a woman has the right to control her body, and therefore should have unilateral control over abortion decisions, the fetus has to be an object, a wart that a woman can get removed – by an obstetrician, not a dermatologist. The fetus can't be a child, a human being, with it's own rights. It has to be an it, not a him or a her. There can't be a Child Protective Services for fetuses.

This takes us into absurd, unresolvable "debates" about when a fetus becomes a human being. Everyone agrees that once it is born, the fetus is now a baby and has full human rights. But when does the transition from fetus to human being occur? The Republican answer is, at conception. The Democrat answer is, we're not exactly sure, but sometime after a woman wants an abortion.

What about during labor? Is abortion OK during labor? No? What about before labor begins? No? OK, what about at 37 weeks? 32? 24? The argument gets stretched back and back, but any cutoff point is arbitrary and is just legislated by special interest groups, except that everyone belongs to a special interest group in this debate. Abortion is in fact murder if a fetus is a human being with full human rights. It's not if the fetus is just a wart. When does the wart become a baby? Round and round it goes.

In a democracy, the legality of abortion gets decided by a vote. Everyone has the right to express their opinion, and to lobby on behalf of their position. But neither side can prove, logically or scientifically, that their team is right. This is good – democracy is good. But how does the "debate" get conducted in America? It's the same problem as in any other "political debate," just a different social issue. Evil Trump is pro-life. Being in favor of life is clearly evil. If you're pro-life, you're anti-women. Well, until the non-aborted fetus is born and happens to be female, then you're pro-women if you protect the female baby, or at least you're pro-future women.

So it's OK to kill women for the convenience of women as long as the women are fetuses. But men should not have the right to interfere with a woman's right to kill her future adult daughter, because that would be anti-women. Hmmm. . . maybe not. Tough one.

As Yoda put it, "Difficult to see, always in motion is the future."

THE OLIVE BRANCH MAYORAL DEBATE

I was unable to acquire the rights to any transcripts of the Trump-Clinton Presidential Debates. However, due to my extensive connections in Canadian media, eh, I was able to acquire a transcript of an unrelated political debate in Canada: The Olive Branch, Ontario Mayoral Debate, recently broadcast in Canada on the Saskabush Provincial Television Network. This debate does not resemble the Trump-Clinton Presidential Debates in any way, not in tone, content, ininity or any other characteristic. It is included here solely for public information purposes.

INT. TELEVISION STAGE.
There are two lecterns on the stage, with a male candidate standing at one and a female candidate at the other.

HOST COMMENTATOR (V.O.)
Welcome to the second debate in the Olive Branch, Ontario Mayoral Election Campaign. Tonight, the candidates will each have 60 seconds to respond to a series of questions selected from submissions by our viewing audience. King Card will respond first and Hilarious Claptrap will respond second. Welcome, candidates.

KING CARD
Thank you, Jeff. And I'd like to thank viewers from our great sister city, Gun Barrel City, Texas, who have tuned in.

HILARIOUS CLAPTRAP
Yes, thank you, Jeff. And thank you viewers for tuning in.

HOST COMMENTATOR (V.O.)
OK, then. First question. What do you plan to do about undocumented immigrants in Olive Branch?

KING CARD
Hang 'em high!

HILARIOUS CLAPTRAP
Well, Jeff, I think we should give people a fair chance. There should be a process.

KING CARD
A process, yeah. Throw a rope over a tree branch works for me.

HOST COMMENTATOR (V.O.)
OK. OK, Mr. Card. Only one response to each question, please. Next question. Do you think New Zealanders pose a security threat?

KING CARD
Definitely. They are way better than us at rugby.

HILARIOUS CLAPTRAP
Who cares about rugby? Anyway, how do you tell the difference between a pig and a hockey mom?

HOST COMMENTATOR (V.O.)
I don't know. How do you tell the difference?

HILARIOUS CLAPTRAP
The hockey mom is wearing lipstick.

KING CARD
I respect women too much to tell a joke like that.

HILARIOUS CLAPTRAP
Yeah, then why did you grab my ass backstage?

KING CARD
I thought we were in a locker room.

HOST COMMENTATOR (V.O.)
OK, candidates. Next question. What do you plan to do to bring jobs back to Olive Branch?

HILARIOUS CLAPTRAP
First of all, I plan to open a Post Office. The citizens of this town have worked hard all their lives. They deserve a Post Office.

KING CARD
Wait a minute. I'm supposed to answer first. That's the problem with these career politicians, always answering questions first but never doing anything. It's all talk, talk, talk.

HILARIOUS CLAPTRAP
Yeah, when you're getting paid $225,000.00 per talk, it pays to talk.

KING CARD
No woman deserves that kind of pay.

HOST COMMENTATOR (V.O.)
Next question. What do you plan to do about dogs peeing on the grass at the public library?

KING CARD
Build a fence.

HILARIOUS CLAPTRAP
The people deserve a dry lawn at their public library. They've worked hard all their lives and they've earned it. I'll apply for a grant from the Federal Library Lawn Revitalization Programme.

KING CARD
Build a fence. Create jobs. Your ideas are hilarious, Hilarious.

HOST COMMENTATOR (V.O.)
Next question. What do you think about the Russians hacking down the crab apple trees at the edge of town?

KING CARD
I have dinner with those guys every Tuesday. Great guys. Love 'em!

HILARIOUS CLAPTRAP
They're trying to destroy our way of life. We've been throwing crab apples at buses every fall since I was a kid.

HOST COMMENTATOR (V.O.)
Watch out, Mrs. Claptrap. You may end up getting investigated by the Olive Branch Police Department.

KING CARD
Terrible. Terrible.

HILARIOUS CLAPTRAP
Well, I never threatened to poop on your porch.

KING CARD
You made me really, really mad. Tweet. Twitter. Twit.

HILARIOUS CLAPTRAP
I'm not a twit.

HOST COMMENTATOR (V.O.)
OK, OK, let's keep this civil. Next question. Do you think New Zealanders should be allowed to play in the National Hockey League?

KING CARD
Definitely not. They don't even own skates. They don't even respect our culture enough to learn how to skate.

HILARIOUS CLAPTRAP
I think there should be a path to the NHL for these people. If they fix their accents and learn how to skate, then I think they should have a chance. A fair

chance.

HOST COMMENTATOR (V.O.)
And what about the top 1%? Have they been paying their fair share? Or would you tax them more?

KING CARD
There are only 378 adult people in Olive Branch, Jeff. Of them, only 169 have finished high school. So the top 1% would be only a couple of people.

HILARIOUS CLAPTRAP
It's time Fred and Mary started paying more taxes. Mary doesn't even bake anything for the bake sale. And last year they went to Florida for five months while we froze our butts off.

KING CARD
Your butt felt fine to me, Hilarious!

HILARIOUS CLAPTRAP
You're quite the card, all right. A King Card in fact.

HOST COMMENTATOR (V.O.)
OK, OK, settle down everybody. Next question. Who do you think will win the Stanley Cup this year?

KING CARD
Better not be one of those foreign teams.

HILARIOUS CLAPTRAP
I think it should be a Canadian team. This great country deserves it, after all the hard work we've done. The people deserve it.

KING CARD
Better not be those Frenchies.

HILARIOUS CLAPTRAP
Hey, my high school boyfriend was French Canadian.

KING CARD
Yeah? You dumped him pretty quick, soon as your future husband got a job at the gas station.

HOST COMMENTATOR (V.O.)
OK, OK. What would you do to make Olive Branch great again?

KING CARD
I'd build a covered hockey rink. Create jobs.

HILARIOUS CLAPTRAP
If we need a covered hockey rink, we can apply to the Federal Covered Hockey Rink Support Programme.

HOST COMMENTATOR (V.O.)
Any other ideas about how to make Olive Branch great gain?

KING CARD
We need to keep them New Zealanders out. Bunch of sheep herders.

HILARIOUS CLAPTRAP
If we allowed more New Zealanders in, we could apply for money from the Federal Sheep Farm Stimulus Programme.

HOST COMMENTATOR (V.O.)
Anything else?

KING CARD
We should see how they do it in Gun Barrel City, Texas. There's a lot of great Christians down there.

HILARIOUS CLAPTRAP
We have our own Christians here.

KING CARD
Yeah, but they're a bunch of pussies.

HILARIOUS CLAPTRAP
I prefer to call them feminists.

KING CARD
Same thing.

HILARIOUS CLAPTRAP
Really, King, are you the king of Olive Branch? Really?

KING CARD
King, king, that's my thing. I wanna be King. No Olive Branch for you. Hilarious!

HILARIOUS CLAPTRAP
The polls say I'll be the winner, so there.

KING CARD
Nyah, nyah.

HILARIOUS CLAPTRAP

That's real grown up, King.

KING CARD
Nobody's going to vote for someone with the name Hilarious Claptrap.

HILARIOUS CLAPTRAP
Yeah, well your grandmother wears Army boots.

HOST COMMENTATOR (V.O.)
OK, OK. Well that wraps up our debate for tonight. We asked the tough questions and the candidates stated their positions clearly. It's up to the voters now. Final comments?

KING CARD
My grandmother was a great Canadian. She deserves nothing but respect.

HILARIOUS CLAPTRAP
All I care about is the people.

HOST COMMENTATOR (V.O.)
OK, well we're out of time. Good night everyone. Thanks for tuning in to this historic debate.

JULIUS J. TURD TAKES A SWIM

Julius was a good friend of mine. We were close - it was like he was inside me. I wanted him to be with me forever, but I knew I had to let him ago. It was hard, but I did.

Like a bird flying from the nest, I had to release him. Julius had to swim in the great sea of life on his own. The last I saw him, he was still treading water – he wasn't going under without a fight. I think of Julius often, but I've never seen him again.

Sure there have been others, but Julius was the biggest friend I ever had. It hurt to let go of him. I've felt empty ever since.

P.S. My Republican friends thought Julius was a Democrat, but my Democrat friends thought he was a Republican.

BERNIE AND THE TOP 1%

Bernie gets my vote for the US Presidential Elections All-American Hypocrisy Prize. He spent his entire campaign railing against the top 1%. The horrible billionaires who have committed the horrible offense of pursuing the American dream and becoming successful. There's nothing more un-American than pursuing the American dream, apparently. He's going to rob the rich and give to the poor just like that romanticized criminal Robin Hood. He's one straight arrow, that Bernie!

Free stuff, kids! You don't have to work for it! It's free! Hooray! Vote for me and you'll get tons of free stuff! College, health care, whatever you want. You won't have to pay for it and your parents won't have to pay for it because the top 1% will foot the bill. What a deal! You don't have to feel guilty about leeching off the top 1% because they are Evil Business Barons. They exploit the workers and laugh all the way to the bank.

Oh, and after your free college and free massages and free whatever else you want, you can still go shop at Walmart – that's where the righteous people shop because everything is cheap there due to being made in China. But we aren't cozying up to China the way Trump does, no siree!

Too bad for Bernie that he wasn't quite able to sell his Top 1% Plan. He came close, but in the end no cigar. When he lost the Democratic nomination, who did he endorse for President? Hillary Clinton. She makes a measly $225,000.00 per talk on Wall Street x dozens of talks. Her net worth is what, somewhere around $100 million? They don't come more top 1% than Hillary.

Hence I nominate Bernie Sanders for the US Presidential Elections All-American Hypocrisy Prize. He earned it.

In Denmark, everyone gets free college education, all Denmarkians plus any other citizens of the EU who wants to go to college in Denmark. I'm not against that as a social policy. But there is no free college in Denmark. It's all paid for through very high personal income tax rates. The idea that you can get endless free stuff because the top 1% is going to pay for it, with no tax increases for "the people," is infantile. I came to the US and took out citizenship, not to get a carbon copy of Canadian social structures, but to be in America, where you can get rewarded for hard work, entrepreneurship and risk taking. Or at least that's the theory.

I'm on Medicare, that free old age social security health care plan. Great! Free stuff! But my free Medicare costs me over $500 a month. I have to pay a higher rate because I still work. I get financially penalized for working and would pay less for my health care if I quit working and started collecting Social Security. Instead, while still contributing to Medicare and Social Security with every paycheck, I get penalized. I doubt if the left wing sees that as un-American, unfair, counter-productive or un-Democratic. And I'm not even in the top 1%. This is how the Free Stuff Plan works – it incentivizes sloth and punishes hard work. If I just sat on my couch all day watching soap operas, and collecting Social Security, the government would stop punishing me financially. Is this really the American way? Is sitting on the couch what made America great? Maybe not, maybe not.

OK, OK I just set myself up. Now the left can attack me for describing people who receive Social Security as sloths on couches. Go for it, boys and girls! The ad hominem attack strategy always beats sitting down and talking about complex social problems, none of which have a quick, easy solution. In Washington, the left is devoting more energy to attacking Trump, calling for investigations and impeachments, and campaigning for 2020 than they are on helping the people. But they sure care about the people. It's the same old partisan gridlock, with the opposite team in the White House. The game rules never change, just the colors of the jerseys worn by the White House team. And boy, talk about great free stuff and benefits and Corporate Board appointments after retirement! Those politicians aren't slouches on couches, that's for sure, Democrats or Republicans.

DEPORTATIONS UNDER THAT RACIST XENOPHOBE, OBAMA

The liberal media flips out about Trump being a racist xenophobe because of his immigration comments and policies. Rant, rail, rant, rail. This is a form of fake news, but it's deniable because the facts are stated correctly. Trump did say this, Trump did say that. Then when Trump counters by saying that the media is biased against him and is putting out fake news, the media is set up for a self-righteous reaction. Fake? What? Only the facts here. And the media is correct, because they did just report the facts, therefore it isn't fake news. But it is fake news. Why?

Fake news isn't mostly about the facts. It's mostly about the spin. Trump said he is going to deport at least 2 million criminals, drug dealers and other assorted undesirables, maybe even 3 million. That's a fact. And how does that fact get reported? Outrage, character attacks, moaning and groaning, Trump is the next Hitler, on and on it goes. There is no calm, rational, balanced discussion of the facts – it's all emotional reactions, outrage and self-righteous posturing.

Could it be a good thing to deport illegal alien drug dealers? Could that be good for America and the beloved people who love Bernie or Hillary? No way, Trump is a fascist – we want to keep all those friendly criminals here, apparently. You would think everyone could agree that it is good to deport violent criminals, gang members and drug dealers. Could we consider focusing on what we agree on as an opening, and then go from there? No way!

The problem is clearly the size and nature of the deportation dragnet. How indiscriminate is it going to be, what will be the total number of deportations, how many children born here to illegal immigrant parents will be included, what is the appeal process? These things can be discussed and negotiated. As we all know, Trump's opening negotiation position, no matter what the subject matter, is always an opening position, just like it is when honest citizens buy a car or a house. This is completely normal human bargaining behavior. And, as we all know, he states his opening position in the bombastic style that got him elected.

If we were really, really interested in a fair solution to the problem of illegal immigrants in America, maybe we could focus not on over-reacting, but on counter-negotiation. The outer reaches of the left wing take the pose of caring about the people, but actually are more invested in hating Trump than on working towards solutions, it seems. That is why all the coverage is on the tear-jerk stories about dreamer kids and bad behavior by ICE and TSA agents. Find the extreme case and pump it for all the anti-Trump mileage you can get out of it.

The fundamental problem is structural and has been going on since before I arrived in America as an immigrant from the old country in 1991. I paid a lot of money for my H1 visa, then my green card, then my citizenship. There are a lot of people on the list for legal immigration. Do we care about them? Do we care when resources get diverted from them to supporting illegal aliens? No, we don't talk about that problem. We just care about the people and hate Trump.

Well, actually, that's not really the problem, it's just a side cost of the fundamental problem. We declare that the illegals are illegal, we catch them and deport them, they come back, and around and around the cycle goes. In the meantime, we run our economy off of illegal aliens, who we don't have to pay much and who don't get any benefits. It's hypocrisy to the Nth degree. We vilify them but employ them – sometimes in reasonable manual labor jobs, sometimes in sweat shops or the sex industry. Or, we romanticize them and try to protect them against Herr Trump. Neither side, Republican or Democrat, has solved the problem, after eight years of Clinton, eight years of Bush, and eight years of Obama.

In fact, Obama deported an average of about 400,000 illegal aliens a year. Why? Because he's a racist xenophobe. Or no, that's not right. He's a wonderful caring humanitarian who was nominated for the Nobel Prize after 11 days in office (he got a lot done in those 11 days). It's Trump who's the racist xenophobe. But let's look at the facts. Not the bipartisan emotions, the facts. According to my high-powered personal computer research, Obama deported over 2 million people during his two terms. The numbers fluctuate a little depending on whether you include only ICE deportations, or deportations by other agencies. But let's go with 2 million as a low-ball estimate.

This means that Evil Trump has to deport at least a million people in his first term just to keep pace with Good Obama. God smiles on Obama and frowns on Trump. And that's why the deportation news is fake news. It's not fake because the facts and Trump quotes are wrong. It's fake because the Obama numbers are not mentioned. Who did Obama say he was going to focus his deportation efforts on? Criminals, violent gang members, drug dealers.

Quiz question: the highest number of deportations in one year were under which of the following US Presidents? Evil Bush 1? Good Clinton? Evil Bush 2? Obama?

The answer: Good Bill Clinton. The husband of Good Hillary Clinton, who in her Presidential race against Evil Trump was endorsed by Good Bernie. Are we all clear on the battle lines?

JOHN KASICH: HOW BORING IS THAT GUY?

Donald Trump killed John Kasich. Wiped the floor with him. Kicked his butt. Beat the crap out of him. It was mano-a-mano in a no-holds-barred, knock down, drag 'em out fight to the finish. Which is peculiar, since dogfights are illegal in America. But the best dog won, that's for sure. Dogs are not allowed to attack each other viciously for the entertainment of a crowd in America, just politicians. It's a dog eat dog world out there, that's for sure. Turns out, Kasich was just dog food for Trump, although he did fight doggedly to the end. In the end, though, he couldn't dog the bullet.

"Doggone it!" said the Kasich supporters.

"That dog is gone!" said the Trump supporters.

For this psychoanalysis, I am not going to consider any of Kasich's policies, just his style and manner.

Kasich had zero chance of winning. He just didn't get the ratings. What? We're going to watch the Housewives of Beverly Hills be polite and reasonable to each other? That ain't no show. We ain't watchin' that shit! No, to get the ratings – sorry, typo, I mean the votes – you have to be an over-the-top TV character, which the Donald literally is. No other politician has a nickname like that. We don't refer to Clinton as the Bill, or Obama as the Barack. They aren't professional wrestlers. I remember my favorite wrestler name growing up in Canada – Hard Boiled Haggarty. Technically, it was my favourite wrestler name, but I don't want to tooth pick the issue. I'm a little long in the tooth for that. I do like to pick nits though, which is called nit picking. This makes sense, because political satirists are nitwits.

How many nits would a nitwit pick if a nitwit could pick nits?

I rest my case. It's too heavy to carry anyway. Nothing like a 24-pack if you're settling in to watch a political debate, though. I happen to have a transcript of a Kasich-Trump debate:

Trump, "He's trying to make America little!"

That's all I have. Sorry. When Kasich was on TV with his family, prior to one of the Republican debates, he seemed like an excellent father, husband and human being. What's really true off camera, I have no idea. But it seemed like John Kasich On Camera might be the same person as John Kasich Off Camera. Then there's the Donald. . . you know it's a TV persona just by the name. Unless Melania calls him The Donald at home, which would be pretty feminist and funny!

It is 100% certain that the Donald who got elected President of the United

States of America was a fake news TV persona. He beat that other fake TV persona, Hillary. The whole thing was fake news even if it was reported accurately.

What did Kasich do that got him beat up by the Donald? He spoke politely. He made reasoned arguments. He made no ad hominem attacks. He looked at both sides of an issue. No wonder he didn't get elected! Who the Hell would want a President like that? The Donald! The Donald! What a great tag team wrestling match it was. The Donald and the Pence versus the Hillary and that other guy whose name I can't remember. The Donald sure threw her to the mat! That's some real wrestling, man! Nothing fake there! How do I know? There was a referee there, making sure the debates were fair, and it was all on TV for everyone to see. Just because Hillary and the Donald were on a stage doesn't mean the whole thing was staged. They each had their own platform shoes. Hillary's heels weren't quite high enough though, so she ended up heeling to the Donald. What a show!

I MADE A BAD CHOICE

I wasn't sure what tone would be suitable for this chapter, so I asked my IPhone. Here is a transcript of the ensuing conversation:

Colin, "Siri, should I try to copy your tone for this chapter?"

Siri, "Yes, Colin, be Siri-ous."

Colin, "OK, serious it is. Thanks, Siri."

This is indeed a very serious topic. All names have been changed to protect the guilty.

I don't recall for sure which state it was, maybe New Jersey, and I'm not sure if it was a State Senator or a Congressman. It goes without saying that he was Republican. The details don't matter because it's always the same story. This married champion of family values had authored a series of bills cracking down on prostitution and other crimes against God. Then he got busted for a DUI. The media found out and he got scorched.

An interesting story? Not really. Let me spice it up. The media found out about the Christian man's arrest because the name of the woman he called to pick him up was broadcast on a police radio band. Reporters were listening in. The woman turned out to be his mistress, not his wife. Now I'm not saying this politician is a hypocrite. He's just a good Christian family man who made a bad choice.

Well, technically, he made three bad choices: to get drunk; to drive drunk; and to call his mistress to pick him up. Well, maybe four bad choices, if we include having a mistress. How do these stories play out? Always the same way. It's like some kind of cultural script. Everybody plays their role perfectly.

First, we have the good Christian family man politician or preacher who stands up for what is right, and loves America, and is a great patriot, and knows that God hates fornicators, homosexuals, sodomites, Democrats, and other human detritus. God is very angry with these derelicts, and He is a just and righteous God, and Lot's wife should have been more obedient, that's for sure. Blah, blah, blah, blah, year in and year out.

What happens next? The good Christian family man gets caught in a hotel room with an underage male hooker, an adult female hooker, his mistress, or some other undesirable sinner. Then he denies that anything like that happened. Then irrefutable evidence is presented on the Evening News. Then the devout Christian holds a press conference and says that he made a bad choice, and we are all sinners, and he has been speaking with his pastor and asking God for forgiveness. Then it comes out that he's had a mistress for years and has been making secret support payments to her because God is against abortion so she had to give birth after he impregnated her. It wasn't the child's fault.

Or, it turns out that multiple under-age prostitutes claim to have done tricks for him. Anyway, then he holds another press conference with his wife to explain that nothing is more important to him than his family, and he is taking some time off to get things right with the Lord. The wife stands stoic in the background because she doesn't want to get turned into a pillar of salt, and the Bible says to stand by your man. She draws the line at having a threesome with her husband's mistress, we think, but then we don't know for sure.

It's very handy to be a good Christian family man because then you can get away with anything – if you're caught you point out that we are all sinners, and vow to get right with God, and then you're good to go! None of your fellow Republicans speak critically of you because they don't know when they're going to get caught.

In the Middle Ages, Catholic monks used to sell indulgences. These were official pieces of paper that you could present at the Pearly Gates when you got there (somehow, a celestial version of the paperwork would be in your hands as you arrived at the Gates). They kept a record of all the purchases in Heaven. If you had purchased enough indulgences, you could get into Heaven for sure, because they paid off your sins, and righted your Holy Balance Sheet. Hole Sheet, man, that's a good scheme, or scam.

These devout family men are textbook cases of reaction formation. Thanks, guys!

ENVIRONMENTAL POLICIES: A EULOGY FOR MOTHER EARTH

Overheard on the pornography film set: "Hurt the bitch! Drill her!"

Overheard at the drilling rig: "Hurt the bitch! Drill her!"

Could it be that Mother Human and Mother Earth get treated the same way by male chauvinist pigs? This is where the Republicans lose me. Ugly attitudes towards the environment are a deal breaker for me. Does The Art of the Deal include treating Mother Earth with reverence? Doesn't seem like it.

While the smart business-savvy Trump Republicans are busy creating jobs and stimulating the economy, and their own bank accounts, what will they do about the environment? Too early to tell yet, but the signs so far don't look good. All these smart business strategies are only smart in the short term. While we're burning through our oil reserves as fast as we can – just look at what the US military consumes – what about the future? Hydrocarbons are good for powering cars and aircraft, but if I remember right, we also use them for other things like plastics. This includes a lot of medical equipment.

I wonder if it would be good policy to conserve this non-renewable resource? Even if we have 100% electronic cars, and airplanes powered some other way, in the future, it would be valuable to have hydrocarbon reserves for plastics, let alone anything else we might want to do with them. Burning the coal, gas and oil at the maximum rate is good for business right now, but what about next century?

In the USA we have historical amnesia in both directions – into the past and into the future. The past doesn't exist, and neither does the future. If I can't see it from my high chair, it ain't there. This is not a grown up way of looking at the world. Since it is apparent that climate change is real, the death of habitat is real, and the death of species is real, there has to be a rationalization strategy in place. When the science says things are looking grim, you can't afford to base your policies on science.

The solution? Climate change is a left wing conspiracy. It's them tree-huggin' liberals, at it again. They don't care about jobs and America. I thought we got rid of the hippies last century. What's up with that? Sup? Yeah man, pinko lefties. That's what I'm talkin' about. If only McCarthy was here to clean up that mess, but they got rid of him too.

Thank goodness we have leftist Hollywood celebrities to protect the environment! Talk about responsible carbon footprints! Their jack boots are responsible for enormous jet setter stimulation of global warming. And how many of them are in the top 1% while supporting Bernie and Hillary?

The environment. The word itself is symptomatic of a spiritual disconnection from Mother Earth. The environment – it's something we can build, modify, and replace at will. Roads are part of the environment. Air pollution is part of the environment. Nature is part of the environment. Rather than expressing, communicating, or requiring any real spiritual connection with the geomagnetic field of the earth (see my book, Human Energy Fields, for an explanation of what I'm talking about), the term the environment reduces everything to a backdrop for business. Now the earth is real estate and trees are either raw materials or tourist enticements. Having to take care of the environment is a nuisance, like having to sweep up the shop floor at the end of the day. If we can sweep everything under the rug and go home after a hard day's work, great. We're making America great again!

Making America great does not seem to involve changing our attitudes towards either human females or Mother Earth.

Let's look in the mirror. The earth-loving Democrats are doing what? Trying to create yet more government regulation in every sphere possible, including Environmental Protection Agency regulations. Throw more regulations and paperwork requirements at the problem – it's a sure-fire solution for everything. But what actually changes in the culture? Nothing. You just have a bigger bureaucracy.

I have never heard a single person campaigning in the primaries, or in the actual Presidential race, mention a single word about a plan to reduce child abuse in America. That is a singular fact. Or not even singular, since N=0. Nada. Not one word. From either side of the aisle. Meanwhile, we're on The Eve of Destruction.

The right wing solution to the problem of child abuse in America (the problem that never gets mentioned) is to bring prayer back into the schools. The left wing solution is more government. But when do we hear the politicians campaigning on a promise to fight child abuse and protect American children from their own parents, uncles and good old Christian grandpas? Oh, I get it – children are not part of the environment. Politicians on both sides of the aisle pretend to care about our children, our most precious resource – oh, whoops! There we go again. Children are a resource, just like coal and gas. We need them for our future factories.

Better ramp up our STEM education so we can compete with the commies in Russia and China down the road! In the meantime, the standards of liberal arts education have declined so far that trash talk can't be differentiated from debate. The Presidential race is a reality TV show. Any idea of looking at the evidence, weighing the arguments, balancing priorities in a complex, dynamic, ever-changing world, or anything of that ilk, is out the window. The whole show is run by emotions and perceptions, with a generous admixture of over-the-top reactions. Republicans think that liberal arts education is partisan, Democratic propaganda, so they're against it, which is yet another symptom of the problem – the failure of liberal arts education impoverishes the intellects of conservatives to the same degree as it does for liberals. Liberal arts education does not equal liberal political policies.

In the meantime, a few isolated tribes in the upper Amazon actually live in and care about "the environment" – but they don't call it the environment, don't look at it as a resource, and don't exploit it for profit. Hello, Republicans and Democrats of the Brave New World. We used to be the environment, hundreds of years ago. We were in it. We were part of it. It was part of us. We had reverence for it. We didn't drill the bitch back then.

By the way, on a completely different topic: the odds of being obsessed with female breasts as an adult male go up if the male was not breast-fed as an infant. To help the American male with this problem, liberated American females get breast implants, just in case the male targeting mechanisms aren't working properly. This helps the male identify the woman he wants to buy jewelry for. Not breast-feeding children in America, then, is a feminist plot to get more jewelry from men. This is how feminists contribute to economic growth. They stimulate the economy by getting breast implants which has the trickle-down effect of stimulating the jewelry industry, which then keeps the shopping malls open, which in turn has a multiplier effect on the real estate market and next thing you know, whiz bam! We need more hotels.

The tree-huggin' women don't participate in this farce. They have a solution: breast-feed your child at least through kindergarten. And no breast implants. Breast implants aren't natural. Naturally, these children are at high risk for being momma's boys and momma's girls in adulthood. But that's good because then they won't watch pornography or work on drilling rigs. Unless they develop reaction formation. See how it's all part of the same dance?

"Come on baby, let's do the twist! Round and around and up and down. Come on, and it goes like this!"

"Basil, Basil, that music is barbaric. Turn it off."

"Quite right, Cecil, quite right. Jolly good point you make there."

BUSHISMS, TRUMPISMS BUT NO OBAMAISMS

George W. Bush said some pretty funny things during his Presidency:

"I'll be long gone before some smart person ever figures out what happened inside this Oval Office." - George W. Bush, Washington, D.C., May 12, 2008

"Anyone engaging in illegal financial transactions will be caught and persecuted." -George W. Bush, Washington, D.C., Sept. 19, 2008

"And they have no disregard for human life." - George W. Bush, on the brutality of Afghan fighters, Washington, D.C., July 15, 2008

"We've got a lot of relations with countries in our neighborhood." - George W. Bush, Kranj, Slovenia, June 10, 2008

"Amnesty means that you've got to pay a price for having been here illegally, and this bill does that." - George W. Bush, on the immigration reform bill, Washington, D.C., June 26, 2007

"The problem with the French is that they don't have a word for entrepreneur."

"If you say you're going to do something and don't do it, that's trustworthiness."

"Justice ought to be fair."

"If the terriers and bariffs are torn down, this economy will grow."

"Reading is the basics for all learning."

I remember being in the Northeast during Bush's second term and going into a small tourist knick-knack shop, which was full of useless junk and a few interesting items. There were multiple collections of Bushisms for sale, and multiple copies of each one. I was in Democrat country. Ha, ha, George Bush, what a Republican idiot! Bad Man, Bad Man. Us no like.

But then there are the other Bushisms, for example:

"Let me start off by saying that in 2000 I said, 'Vote for me. I'm an agent of change.' In 2004, I said, 'I'm not interested in change - I want to continue as president.' Every candidate has got to say 'change.' That's what the American people expect." - George W. Bush, Washington, D.C., March 5, 2008

That sounds like honesty and integrity to me. Also, George Bush is a very funny guy, for example:

"Bush goes to Hel. That's what a lot of people want." - George W. Bush, on his visit to the Hel Peninsula, Gdansk, Poland.

Some Bushisms are classical examples of dyslexia – "terriers and bariffs" being one. The collectors of Bushisms, then, are mocking George Bush because he has a handicap, because he has dyslexia. This is perfectly acceptable in left wing circles. But imagine if Donald Trump mocked a handicapped person by imitating his physical disability, like he did when imitating a reporter with an impaired arm. Then the howls would go up, which they did! It's a double standard. And this standard is standard operating procedure on the left, including in the left-leaning media.

It's another variation on the fake news problem. In this example, Trump did in fact imitate a reporter's disability, and that in fact was crass and tasteless behavior by Trump. The fake news is the failure to comment in a balanced fashion on people who mocked George W. Bush for his dyslexia. Not all Bushisms were based on dyslexia, and some were just absurd statements, but still, the double standard rules the day. Then we get over-generalization against Trump – he's all bad, crass and a buffoon - and no mention at all of any failings on the left. The people on the left are the Good People, so they don't get attacked.

And then what happens? As always, Donald Trump over-reacts to an accusation by the left, which then justifies the left in over-reacting against him, and on and on it goes. Each side is vindicated and justified by the extremism of the opposing side. Why do we never see any Obamaisms in the media? For two reasons: 1) Obama is more measured, articulate and reasonable in style than Trump, so he doesn't make outrageous remarks, and 2) he wouldn't get trashed by the left wing media even if he did.

JUSTIN TRUDEAU AND DONALD TRUMP SMOKE THE PEACE PIPE

On February 12, Anno Domini 2017, at the White House, Prime Minister Justin Trudeau of Canada and President Donald Trump of the United States of America held a joint press conference. It would be hard to find two leaders of the western world who are more different in tone, style and manner, or in policy. Yet how did they behave, both of them? With decorum, with a serious tone, politely. To me, this press conference should be the model for the Trump Card. Both men acted like leaders. Neither kowtowed to the other. Both acknowledged that they have differences in policy, and neither man demonized the other.

Both men focused on what they, and their two countries have in common, what their common interests are, and how the two countries can work together for the common good of both. Both referred to a long history of mutual support and respect.

If Americans would behave like Justin Trudeau and Donald Trump did at that press conference, the world would become a better place. Why can't that happen? Because the right knows that Justin Trudeau is just a granola-eating, yoga-practicing Commie and is soft on terror. The left knows that the Donald is actually the Adolph, with a funny bird sitting on his head. Why should those two parties party with each other?

Quiz question: Colin A. Ross, M.D. currently holds two valid passports, one from Canada and one from the United States of America; which country has he betrayed? Maybe neither, maybe, maybe. . . on the other hand, you have to wonder what those two guys were smoking, at their joint press conference. It definitely didn't look like a drunken bar fight, which is why alcohol is legal in both Canada and America. Peace, man.

RIDICULOUS BODY LANGUAGE ANALYSES

All around the mulberry bush
The monkey chased the weasel
The monkey thought 'twas all in fun
Pop goes the weasel!

Of all the ridiculous experts on all the cable TV talk talk talk shows, in my professional opinion as an M.D. psychiatrist and as a legend in my own mind, I'd say that the body language analysis clowns take the cake. They play their analyses as if they're providing us with some kind of scientific insight, when really they're just responding to the Trump Card in the Rorschach Ink Blot Test.

For example, out of the thousands of photos of Donald and Melania Trump, the interviewer, who is unbiased and only interested in the facts, shows the objective expert a photo of Melania slightly behind her husband with an unhappy look on her face. This then becomes the proof that the Donald is a controlling chauvinist and Melania is unhappily married. But it's one photo out of thousands. What about the expert's scientific analysis of the dozens of photos in which Melania looks perfectly happy? Anyway, who wouldn't frown once in a while having to attend all those events and photo ops?

The analyst who takes the biggest cake, again in my professional opinion, is the clown who commented on the handshake between Donald Trump and Justin Trudeau. It was a quick exchange as Trudeau got out of a car, shook hands and entered a doorway. The expert could tell, due to his highly trained shmexpertise, that the Donald's body language told everything. Trump was asserting male dominance, for sure. The proof was right there. The unbiased media ate up the cake, with only a little icing and a few crumbs dribbling down onto their chins and then onto their well-laundered shirts.

Get out a tissue, and cry for America.

Ring around the rosie
A pocket full of posies
Atishoo atishoo
We all fall down!

GUN POLICIES: AMERICA AND HER BOYFRIEND KALASHNIKOV

"Yo, America, you momma so fat she got her own zip code."

"Don't diss America, man, she hot!"

"She hot, all right."

"Her man Kalashnikov will get in your face, man. See what I'm sayin'?"

"Yeah. I'm cool. Where she live?"

"One block north of her uncle Mex."

"OK, if I'm around there, America, I'll look you up."

"Careful, man. She hot but she mean."

Now that I've given myself fair warning, I'll proceed. But first I want to make a few points about the Constitution of the United States, which became law in 1789. The first ten Amendments of the Constitution are known as the Bill of Rights. But there are 27 in total. Amendments 13, 14 and 15 are known as the Reconstruction Amendments and were approved from 1865 to1870. Amendment 13 abolished slavery in 1865. Prior to 1865, slavery was legal in the United States, and the right to own slaves was protected by the Constitution.

The reason for the history lesson, is that there are Constitutional fundamentalists in America who see the Constitution as being almost like the Bible, which, as we know, is the direct word of God. The Constitution is the inviolable word of the Founding Fathers, who are as close to being God as any human beings have ever, ever gotten, not counting Our Lord Jesus Christ. Constitutional fundamentalists view the constitution as an immutable, holy document that provides ultimate guidance and authority on all things, or at least quite a few things. There is no questioning the Constitution according to the fundamentalists.

Constitutional fundamentalists permit only a literal interpretation of the Constitution, which is the revealed truth from the Founding Fathers. In fact the Constitution is a secular political document that was written by a group of politicians. You can't trust politicians, except the politicians who wrote the Constitution.

Let's set that contradiction in attitudes towards politicians aside. I'm not in any way against the Constitution, but it is not Immutable Revealed Truth. In fact, there are 27 Amendments to the Constitution, and the 27th was passed in

1992, over 200 years after 1789. So, the Constitution is not immutable, and it can and has been changed.

The Second Amendment reads:

A well regulated militia being necessary to the security of a free state, the right of the people to keep and bear arms shall not be infringed.

The point here is the types of arms that were available in 1789. People having muskets at home seems OK to me. In Canada, I owned a rifle and a shotgun. But is the intent of the Second Amendment really to permit people to own weapons of mass destruction? Let's walk it up the chain: shotguns, check; rifles, check; machine guns, check; bazookas, check; tanks, check; smart bombs, check; nuclear bombs, check. Is there any cutoff point? Does it really make sense to interpret the Second Amendment to mean that private citizens should be able to own nuclear weapons? America is the only country in the world where private citizens owning nuclear weapons needs to be debated.

The primary rationalization for owning AK-47's and Kalashnikovs is protection of oneself and one's family. If a burglar breaks into your home, he's definitely going to give you enough time to go to your gun safe, get out your AK-47, load it, and pump a couple of dozen rounds into him, so that makes sense. And if the bad People = the Communists, ever take over the government, you can sure as heck hole up on your homestead and fight off the US military, which will be controlled by the Communist government that has taken over, which almost happened during the Obama administration, but we don't have to worry about that for the next four years.

Arguments and facts play no role in the "gun debate" in America. Questioning the Second Amendment is pretty much like questioning the Bible, which definitely says Lot's wife deserved what she got. What if it's a fact that having guns in your home increases your risk of being killed by a gun? Irrelevant. Anyway, guns don't kill people, people kill people. So don't regulate guns. If a car goes over the speed limit, you don't give the car a ticket. True. But irrelevant.

This is another example of political polarization in America. If Obama suggests that we consider amending the Second Amendment, he must be against the Constitution and therefore against freedom and democracy and This Great Country. That pretty much proves he's a Communist. But why would it be un-American to amend the Second Amendment? Couldn't America just decide to do that, if it is a democracy? Why? I don't get it. We've done other Amendments over the years. But then, I grew up in the Old Country, so it's not surprising that I don't understand.

There is no possibility of a reasonable gun debate in America. It just is not going to happen. Problem is, guns are only one topic out of many on which there is no possibility of a reasoned debate or discussion. It's the Shootout at the OK Corral every time. That's what's wrong with America – Trump is just a symptom of the problem. Attacking a symptom will never fix the problem. The problem will persist beyond the one or two terms of Trump's presidency, just like it persisted beyond those dark days known in history as the Obama Age. The elders are still talking about those days, because they were there, and they remember.

GUNS AND MENTAL ILLNESS

I'm a psychiatrist, so I get to sound off on this topic if I want. In fact I already did:

Ross, C.A. (2014). Gun control and mental illness. Journal of Trauma and Treatment, 3, 203.

Concerning guns and mental illness, my beef is mostly with the right wing but also, surprisingly, with a lot of left wing people who want to take guns away from the mentally ill. As always, the "debate" about guns and the mentally ill is not based on a reasonable analysis of the facts, among politicians or the voters. The politicians have been voted in by the voters, by the way.

We have to take the guns away from those crazies! That's how we're gonna make America safe! That's the usual rant. But what are the facts? All authorities, all research studies, are in overwhelming agreement on the main point: the rate of gun violence in people with serious mental disorders is no different from the rate in the general population. Even if it's a hair greater in some studies, this is all due to substance abuse, statistically, not to schizophrenia or bipolar disorder or other serious mental disorders. This basic fact should silence "the conversation" but it doesn't.

If the seriously mentally ill are at no greater risk for gun violence than the general population, which is a fact, then it makes no sense to take away their right to own guns. This in itself would be a violation of the Constitution and would, you would think, require an amendment to the Second Amendment, which the right wing people who want to take the guns away from the crazies are totally against, on the grounds that the Holy Founding Fathers wrote the Bill of Rights. The Constitution is what makes America Great! Or at least it used to make America Great – apparently we had a lapse into non-Greatness, otherwise we wouldn't need to Make America Great Again. But never mind, we're Great anyway.

To repeat: taking away the right of any segment of the populace to own guns is a violation of the Second Amendment.

In any case, how would we implement a policy to take away guns from the crazies? We would have to screen the entire populace with standardized psychiatric interviews in order to identify all the seriously mentally ill people. This would be an invasion of privacy, which if I remember right is protected by the Fourth Amendment of the Constitution, which prohibits unlawful search and seizure. Imagine how much that would cost, all the legal challenges it would provoke, and the logistical nightmare of doing all the interviews and forcing people to open their doors. . . if a person refused to be interviewed, would they be arrested? For what crime?

If we didn't interview everybody, then we would have to take gun rights away from people who are already diagnosed, but to do this we would have to violate their right to privacy of medical records. Back to the legal challenges and costs problem. But even if we did let Big Brother review everybody's medical records, and took the guns away from the diagnosed crazies, we would be penalizing people with mental disorders who were getting treatment, and rewarding those who avoid treatment. Does that make sense?

People who want to take guns away from the mentally ill sometimes use the word crazies – I don't, except here, to satirize the stupidity of the term. But who are we talking about when we talk about the mentally ill? Mental illness is a very broad category that includes spider phobias, bulimia, and PTSD – how about taking guns away from veterans with PTSD? How would that fly politically? Not well, I imagine. OK, so we would exclude angry, bitter soldiers with PTSD who we know have elevated rates of gun suicide from our gun control plan – but why? Their risk is higher than the general population. Well, I guess we have to target only the politically correct disorders, like schizophrenia. No one talks about these implementation problems.

Hey, I have a great idea! Let's identify a segment of the population that is actually at increased risk of gun violence and take the guns away from them! How about inner city black males between 15 and 30 years of age? We can get the white middle-aged politicians to push that through and the ACLU should be fine with it because we're protecting Americans, right? I don't think so. That would be racial profiling and racial discrimination, not to mention age discrimination. That was fine in the nineteenth century, before that pesky Thirteenth Amendment was passed, but not here in the enlightened twenty-first century.

In my opinion, taking guns away from the mentally ill is equally as repugnant as talking them away from black males. But the mentally ill seem to be a politically acceptable target – it's OK to discriminate against them because they're mentally black. It's not the color of their skins, it's the color of their brains that gets us scared. This is doubly stupid because it's discrimination plus it would have no effect on gun death rates in America – homeless mentally ill people killing white people in suburbia? I don't think so.

In the end, it's politicians huffing and puffing to make it look like they're doing something to protect the voters. They can target the mentally ill with political impunity and don't have to worry about reducing gun sales, which would rile up those gun-toting NRA voters. That's the bottom line anyway, gun sales. All the rest is just huff and puff and distraction.

You think there might be some stigma against mental illness in America? Maybe, given that they're the only group in America for whom we can even suggest taking away their guns, even if they've committed no crimes. We would be preventing future crimes. Let me conclude with some arithmetic:

Let's say our focus is on mass shootings, some of which have been perpetrated by people with diagnosed severe mental disorders. Let's say we want to take the guns away from everyone with schizophrenia. . . there has never been a female mass shooter so we can forget about the women. Most shooters are between 15 and 30. If you take out your calculator and punch in the numbers, it comes out to roughly 100,000 males between 15 and 30 with schizophrenia in America. How many of the mass shooters of the last two decades have had diagnosed schizophrenia? A handful. Psychiatrists have zero ability to predict which person is going to become a mass shooter, so no amount of screening would identify these people in advance. Some of them have seen a psychiatrist prior to their shootings, which proves the point.

We're going to take guns away from 100,000 citizens in order to take them away from a handful of future crime perpetrators? Again, how about taking guns away from 100,000 black males in Chicago and other inner cities? Outrage, outrage, outrage! Outrage from the left, for sure. What does the right have to say about it? The criminals will just get illegal guns on the street anyway – it's not guns that kill people, it's criminals. OK, fine, then why take guns away from the mentally ill?

Every once in a while, in a therapy group, the subject of stigma about mental illness comes up. The people I work with have been hit hard with stigma. Their mental disorders are clearly tied into their childhood trauma. I always tell them that actually, in my opinion, the so-called mentally ill people who come for treatment are often the healthiest members of their families. The perpetrators are in denial and are out there acting as if they're the normal ones. The perpetrators fail to inform the citizenry that they are perpetrators but, if the family secret of a mentally ill child is revealed, they will say what a shame it is that their child has a biological brain disease.

THE FASCISM TIPPING POINT: THE LEFT'S TURN

In 1991, I was working as a psychiatrist in Winnipeg, Canada when I began to seriously consider moving to the United States – but I changed my mind and moved to Texas instead.

Since arriving in Texas, I have been concerned about America's potential to turn into a fascist state. This concern increased a little bit year by year after 9/11. During the Bush and Obama administrations, I was mainly concerned that the US might become a right-wing fascist state. I remember one God-fearing Republican politician who proposed building a large enclosure with a high fence and placing all the gay and lesbian people in America inside the fence. They would eventually die out since they don't have heterosexual sex, he reasoned, and America would be rid of that category of sinners.

Besides being fascist, insane, inhuman and criminal (just some minor drawbacks in the plan) this proposal is scientifically stupid, because homosexuality is not inherited, there is no gene or set of genes for homosexuality, and the dang gay people would just pop up in the next generation, bred into existence by God-fearing, married, good Christian couples, plus atheist couples, Muslim couples, etc., etc.

In a right-wing Christian fascist state, the following Crimes Against God would be prohibited by law: married woman keeping their maiden names; abortion; anal intercourse; oral sex; homosexuality; being trans-gendered; abortion; endorsing the reality of global warming; teaching evolution in schools; and sundry other anti-Biblical activities too numerous to mention. Prayer would be mandatory in schools, forget about wearing a turban or a hijab, and forget about any school kids taking one of those Jewish holidays. Note, however, that My God is a Jewish Carpenter is a popular decal placed on the backs of SUVs in Texas, along with stickers declaring that My Child is An Honor Student at _____.

As the far right wing Christian fundamentalists tried to take control of the Republican party, it became clear over the course of the Bush administration that they weren't going to succeed. Losing to Obama twice really beat them down (thank God!). I gradually became less and less concerned about tipping the cow over into right wing fascism.

Then something bizarre and strange happened: Donald Trump entered the race. Over the course of the primaries, and the Republican debates, the Donald and Mike Versus Hillary and What's His Name tag team wrestling matches became more and more and more. . . more whatever. Not too gradually, my concern shifted to the opposite political pole. Now I'm concerned about America tipping over into a left-wing fascist political state. I don't lose any sleep over this, and I don't think it's actually going to happen, but that's the way the cow is leaning right now.

Here is a tip for America: we aren't that far away from a tipping point and what we see in public is just the tip of the iceberg, because most of the fascist energy is seething in the unconscious mind. If those demons come up from Hell, watch out! As an irrelevant aside, I just read my maternal grandfather's account of being a summer student Protestant minister in rural Quebec over 100 years ago. He got the evil eye from the Catholics in the vicinity. They believed that fireflies were actually demons, and fearfully avoided them. When a bridge collapsed, they blamed the Prime Minister, and he was voted out in the next election – as if a leader of a country is personally responsible for all civil engineering mishaps in the country, and has the power to foresee and prevent them. It's not grown-up thinking.

The thought processes are the same in the Era of Trump in the United States of America, pretty much. An example: the President has the ability to influence and control gas prices at the pump. That is a superstition, an example of primitive magical thinking. No President has the power of Santa Claus. Presidents can't ride in the sky in sleighs pulled by reindeer, for crying out loud! Get real.

What would happen if the extreme left established a fascist state in America? There would be Re-Education Camps for misguided citizens who disagreed with Big Sister, just like there were during the Cultural Revolution in China. Now, I've actually spoken with people whose parents were interred in Re-Education Camps in China, and I am a coauthor on published papers with some of them, based on my trips to Shanghai Mental Health Center. I know what Maoist Re-Education Camps do to people, and it ain't pretty.

What would get you sent to Camp in a left-wing Feminist Fascist state? Questioning a woman's right to abortion; questioning whether homosexuality is OK; supporting Donald Trump; believing that the Bible is the word of God. We know that Satan is the Father of Lies, but when you look in the mirror what do you see, Ms Feminist Re-Educator? The wonderful feminist living in the surface of your mind, or the evil demon lurking in your subconscious? When you look at the Trump Card, what do you see? Oh, Hell gets a little closer then, eh!

From a psychoanalytical perspective, Hell is just a metaphor for the subconscious mind. It isn't really demons that are lurking down there, it's Evil Id Impulses. The Imps of the unconscious are catalogued in DSM-5 in the section called Impulse Control Disorders. These disorders occur when the Church can't keep the evil demans – I mean demons – down. Ever take a walk on the top of the Duomo in Milan? Demons everywhere, gargoyles, lewd creatures, all commissioned by the Divine Bureaucracy of the Catholic Church. Seems like the Divine Fathers were somewhat obsessed with the Hell-Shemons, I mean nuns, and wanted to go down on them, I mean down to them. A brief walk in Hell can be swell, if you mean well, said the man who fell from grace, but put his face where he wanted, on Grace, in the fires of Hell, which burn hot, and smell kind of like sulfur, but there's some good tail down there and hail that! Heil Hell!

There seems to be a degree of turbulence in the human psyche. A few subconscious conflicts here and there. Nothing to worry about, though. By the way, I was recently assigned to a Feminist Re-Education Camp due to a paper I published in the Journal of Child Sexual Abuse. I wrote a paper on problems in the Sexual Disorders sections of DSM-III (1980), DSM-IV (1994) and DSM-5 (2013). I also wrote similar papers on DSM-5 and autism, schizophrenia, dissociative disorders, somatic symptom disorders, obsessive compulsive and delusional disorders. The only paper that brought up the licking hot flames of Feminist Hell was the one on sexual disorders. Justice will be done.

Two spherical object compressing likely lesbian feminist learned colleagues wrote in to the journal about my paper. Now, before proceeding I have to advise the Court that in none of these papers critiquing DSM-5 did I express any personal opinions about any of these disorders. The purpose of the papers was to point out errors of logic, contradictions and inconsistencies in various sections of the manual. Debating these matters is fine.

In my paper about the sexual disorders sections, I discussed homosexuality, gender identity disorder (now gender dysphoria in DSM-5), frotteurism and other disorders that have been included in various editions of the DSM, meaning that the American Psychiatric Association officially considered them to be mental disorders. I never expressed any personal opinions on any of the DSM disorders. Consequently I was sentenced to being burned at the stake by my two colleagues.

Neither of my two esteemed colleagues discussed any of the contradictions and inconsistencies I had pointed out in DSM-III, DSM-IV and DSM-5. Instead they attacked me personally. At the Re-education Camp I learned that I am a dinosaur, a male chauvinist pig, and intellectually incompetent, since I can't even grasp the difference between sexual orientation and gender identity. They said my attitudes were from the 1950's, which in their vocabulary means the Dark Ages, or at least the Trump Ages. By the way, sexual orientation means who you want to have sex with; gender identity means what sex you are when you have sex with the gender you want to have sex with.

This is how Feminist Fascism operates. If the Thought Police catch even the faintest whiff of heresy, it's off to the Camp with you, or worse, Off With Your Head! It's the same kind of fundamentalism, intolerance, social control, and idealization-devaluation as we see in borderline personality disorder, and in right-wing extremists. If I behaved like my two colleagues, I would have responded by calling them a pair of borderline bitches, but I didn't sink to their level. Instead I made a reasoned, scholarly response, and pointed out with quotations and citations from my original paper and their critique that they had misunderstood my paper: it focused entirely on problems in DSM-5 and its predecessors, and no personal opinions or attitudes of mine were expressed in it.

This is how such spherical object compressing feminists behave when writing in academic journals. Imagine the moves they would use in a street fight! Another irrelevant aside: a standard model for understanding political extremism is the horseshoe model. According to this model, the political spectrum is like a horseshoe: the two extreme ends of the horseshoe are closer to each other than either is to the middle. I like that model: you can kick ass with it, cut through the horseshit, and tell it like it is. Praise the Lord, however you understand Her while working Step One.

No need to make amends, however, not now, feminist colleague sisters – that comes later on, like maybe Step Four or Step Six or something. Watch out you don't get goosed while goose-stepping through your recovery, though. That's a hazard when you're a single American woman in Italy. I remember when my family moved to Sicily in the sixties – my 12-year old sister couldn't go on the bus alone because she would be fondled and pinched by adult Italian men. That Dodge definitely needed some feminist cleanup. Heil Helen!

Ross, C.A. (2013). Biology and genetics in DSM-5. Ethical Human Psychology and Psychiatry, 15, 195-198.

Ross, C.A. (2014). Problems with the psychosis section of DSM-5. Psychosis, 6, 235-241.

Ross, C.A. (2014). Problems with autism, catatonia and schizophrenia in DSM-5. Schizophrenia Research, 158, 264-265.

Ross, C.A. (2015). Commentary: Problems with the sexual disorders sections of DSM-5. Journal of Child Sexual Abuse, 24, 195-201.

Ross, C.A. (2015). Trauma and aggression in DSM-5. Journal of Trauma, Maltreatment and Aggression, 24, 484-486.

Ross, C.A. (2015). Problems with DSM-5 somatic symptom disorder. Journal of Trauma and Dissociation, 16, 341-8.

BIG BEAUTIFUL PHARMA LIKE YOU'VE NEVER SEEN BEFORE

There is a person in Idaho who is a very bad person. I haven't met him, and I don't know anything about him, and I've never spoken to anyone who ever met him. So how do I know he's bad? Donald Trump endorsed him. Similarly, I know that the Health Care that Trump will introduce will be very bad for America, bad, bad, bad. However, I don't actually know anything about that Health Care. I have no idea who it covers, what the premiums and deductibles are, or anything else about it. I just know it's bad because Donald Trump endorsed it.

This was the left wing position on Trump's health care reform during the first two months of his Presidency. They knew it was bad without knowing anything about it. Trumpcare could be worse than Obamacare in some ways, and better in some ways. It could be a disaster. It could be a big improvement. That's all we knew after the first two months, so how could anyone have an intelligent opinion? Just because someone is intelligent, doesn't mean that her opinions are necessarily intelligent. Lack of facts is no reason not to have an opinion, however, because we know that everything Trump will do during his Presidency will be bad and wrong. We know this because we don't like his ties and his wife is way too gorgeous, which is very offensive to feminists.

How about Big Pharma? What will Trump do about that blight? Well, let's look at history starting with the beginning of the Obama Era and going up to Trump's inauguration. Under the Obama regime, what was true? Big Pharma made gigantic profits. Big Pharma over-billed Medicare by billions of dollars. Big Pharma lobbied Congress and the Senate at a cost of hundreds of millions or billions over eight years. Big Pharma settled a large series of combined criminal and civil cases brought against them by the Obama government, the largest reaching $2 billion, and carried on with business as usual. In the meantime, Hillary Clinton was getting paid $225,000 per talk for dozens of talks on Wall Street. However, due to her integrity and love of The People, none of this money influenced her in any way. Big Pharma, Big Insurance, Big Oil, they were all just being generous to Hillary because she's a Good Person.

The left wing and the left wing media were silent about all this, and they thought Obama getting nominated for a Nobel Peace Prize after 11 days in office made perfect sense. Obama was a great President for Big Pharma. Let's hope the Donald doesn't mess up and change that! Wouldn't want any health care reform there.

Let's diverge on our psychoanalytical path for a moment. What about Obamacare? I know a 61-year old single woman who is healthy, takes no prescription medications, has no chronic diseases, exercises regularly, does not smoke, and has a pretty healthy diet. Her employer stopped providing assistance with her health insurance so she had to go on Obamacare. Under wonderful caring-for-the-people Obama, her insurance premiums were about $440 a month in 2015. In 2016 they went up to about $540. In 2017, her monthly premium was going to be $775 a month with a deductible of $6850. This was an HMO policy, which was the only kind offered, so she had to change her doctors.

As a result, this woman got out of Obamacare starting in January, 2017. In her state, Texas, it was illegal for insurers to offer year-round non-Obamacare health insurance, so she had to buy a so-called short-term policy that was only good for 360 days. However, as a result of not having insurance for 365 days in 2017, she was going to have to pay the Federal Government of the United States of Obama a fine of $2200. No way we would want to reform that health care plan! Bad Donald, bad Donald!

If we assume that the woman in the illustration made about $60,000 a year, then $770 x 12 = $9240 a year were her insurance costs = 15.4% of her gross income. If $50,000, then 18.5% and so on. This is a middle class working woman by any economic standards, the very class that Barack and Hillary and Bernie swore they would represent and protect. They forgot to protect the middle class from Big Government.

For those who don't live in our Great Country, a health care deductible of $6850 means that you have to pay 100% of your first $6850 of medical expenses in a calendar year out of your own pocket. You don't really have health care insurance unless something really bad happens, even though you have health insurance. Even then, you still have a co-pay, which means you have to pay a percentage of all your medical bills out of your pocket, even after meeting your deductible. An HMO is a Health Maintenance Organization – this means that your Obamacare will only pay for treatment by a very restricted list of doctors and hospitals. This, despite Obama's promising over and over and over that no one would have to change doctors under the Affordable Care Act. The Affordable Care Act – what a joke of a name!

Back to the Pharma. Or, no, let's go to student loans in the United States for a minute. Student loans were a major profit center for the Federal Government throughout the Obama administration. Interest rates for student loans charged and collected by Obama varied between 8% and 8.5%, far above the lending rate of the evil corporations or the evil mortgage companies. Vote for Hillary! Vote for Bernie! Vote for Barack! They'll protect you from the evil corporations! While we're cheering, let's ignore the fact that no other Big Business in America financially exploited American youth to anywhere near the level of the Obama government. Sorry folks, these are just facts.

OK, Big Pharma. At Pharmer's we know a thing or two about Pharma, because we've seen a thing or two. Take the statins. In two recent meta-analyses published in mainstream medical journals, the finding was that statins have no effect on all-cause mortality. What is a meta-analyses? This is when you gather up all the existing studies, pool them, and analyze the overall results from all these studies. What is all-cause mortality? That means death from all causes. The results of the meta-analyses prove that if you take a statin, you don't actually live any longer – your cholesterol will go down some and you will have somewhat fewer heart attacks, but you won't actually live longer.

These are the medical, scientific facts. Does your doctor explain this to you? Does the drug company mention the facts in their TV ads, or during their marketing visits to your doctor? Hard to do that when you're so busy running to the bank to deposit the billions of dollars you make off of statins every year. Notice I haven't even entered side effects of statins into the cost-benefit calculation.

How about antidepressants, another multi-billion dollar class of medications? Meta-analyses show conclusively that if you gather up all the studies, including those that were not published or were suppressed by the drug companies, antidepressants are at most only a tiny bit more effective than placebo. A tiny bit. On a depression scale that ranges from a score of zero to over 50, at the end of the studies, when you average them all together, the difference between antidepressant and placebo is under 2 points. Does your doctor mention this while he is writing out your prescription?

This was the state of affairs under Obama. The drug companies applauded all the way to the bank every year. And we're concerned that Trump might be bad for American health care? He might, but let's be real about the State of the Union under Obama before we start firing mortar rounds at the Trump White House. Well, not firing mortar rounds but maybe marching on Washington and burning our bras in protest.

Trump did say he's going to force Big Pharma to drastically reduce Medicare drug costs. Maybe he will, maybe he won't, but how about if we wait and see before we condemn him? Oh, and what about direct-to-consumer advertising by drug companies? Which countries on Planet Earth allow drug companies to advertise on TV? The United States of America, Brazil and New Zealand. All other countries in the world have banned this practice. Hurray! Go America! Go Obama! Go Big Pharma! What a Country! Obama sure made peace with the drug companies. Maybe that's why he got the Nobel Peace Prize. And you consumers bought all of this, and thought you were being protected by the Good Father in the Big White House? Looks like you got what you voted for.

It's OK, it's OK, you're safe. You can rely on the mainstream media to give you the real news. Billions of dollars in drug ads aren't going to influence them at all. They are independent journalists. You can rely on them for the accurate news about drugs.

"I'm so glad to hear that, Basil. I'll sleep well tonight."

"Yes, so will I, my good fellow, so will I."

"Good night moon."

MARY JANE AND THE WAR ON DRUGS

How about if we go back in time and try an experiment? What shall we call it? How about Prohibition? Prohibition will be good because it will reduce the amount of drinking, which will reduce the amount of gambling and fornicating, and help to bring America back to the Lord.

Now back to the future, which is actually the present. What happened during Prohibition? Al Capone made a lot of money. People got killed in the streets. Corruption was rampant. We already know what happens when we make alcohol illegal. What happens when we make marijuana illegal? We create an economy in which the drug cartels have so much cash they can't launder it all and have to store it on pallets in warehouses. We create gang violence, gun violence, and all kinds of robberies by people who are trying to raise some drug money. Add on heroin and cocaine and you've got a disaster in America. Not to mention the rest of the world.

Prohibition of marijuana is good for business, though. The people who profit off it are the cartels, the jails, and the lawyers. Who pays for the law enforcement, legal system and prison expenses of the war on drugs? The people who voted for Bill Clinton, George Bush, Barack Obama and Donald Trump, plus the people who voted for the losers in all those elections. There are plenty of voters, in fact there's one born every minute.

I remember in medical school hearing dire warnings about reefer madness and how marijuana is a gateway drug, and how bad it is for your health. Clearly, smoking either marijuana or regular cigarettes is not good for your lungs. But that's not the point. Marijuana is not more harmful than alcohol, biologically, medically or scientifically. Yet my Professors condemned marijuana very strongly, while being completely permissive concerning alcohol. Every medical student saw cases of end-stage alcoholism. I saw young people vomiting blood from esophageal varices, young people in coma from alcohol-induced liver failure, and young people in the morgue.

No one, not one doctor had ever treated a case of serious disease caused by marijuana. No one had ever heard of a case of someone killed by a driver stoned on marijuana (although I'm sure that happens occasionally). But the attitudes were very, very extreme: marijuana was all bad, and alcohol was and should be legal. The dire warnings about marijuana being a gateway drug were never accompanied by warnings about alcohol being a gateway drug. This was all based on attitude, not science.

Similarly, I heard doctors pontificating about how evil a drug heroin is – we weren't talking about heroin destroying America because I was still in Canada, but there was already a big heroin problem in Vancouver. I listened to conversations in which a doctor insisted that heroin is bad, bad, bad, much worse than the opiates I saw in gallon jugs in the nursing stations on the cancer ward. The doctor believed that even if it was legal and prescribed by doctors, heroin would cause far more addiction and problems than the other opiates he prescribed without hesitation. It just wasn't scientifically true. I guarantee y'all that if we did a double-blind study, neither doctor nor patient could tell who was on heroin and who was on Dilaudid, if we prescribed equivalent doses. All the opiates interact with the same receptors in the brain.

So little reason and so much emotion, so much projection. And I'm talking about the medical profession. The medical profession's version of the war on drugs is a war on brain abnormalities. It is certain that years of heavy meth usage can damage your brain. That is simply a scientific fact. But that's not what doctors, including psychiatrists, mean when they say that substance abuse is a brain disease. They mean that you had a genetic brain disease that caused you start abusing substances and get hooked on them. The abnormality was present before the drugs were first taken.

This is such a bogus model that I'm not even going to debate it here. Strangely, it is endorsed by people on both the left and the right. What is Trump's attitude towards substance abuse? We don't really know yet. It could be that he buys the disease model of substance abuse. Maybe he will go for the military model, or maybe he thinks that it's a failure of morals and character, and can be treated with a return to Christian family values. I'm still waiting for any politician of any stripe to talk about substance abuse in a way that makes sense to me. So far, no one to vote for on that issue.

I had a classmate in medical school who was a real fun guy. One day I saw him drinking beer at the top of the lecture hall, during a lecture. Everybody sure thought that was funny! Some years later he became an anesthetist and died of an overdose of anesthesia drugs. Maybe instead of a war on drugs, we should be focused on the demand side of the problem, not with punitive, legal or military measures, but with social and psychological support. In 2001, Portugal greatly reduced the legal consequences for possessing recreational amounts of street drugs, combined with needle exchange programs, enhanced access to treatment, methadone programs and a set of related measures, and their drug problem dropped dramatically by a number of different measures including new cases of HIV among drug users and drug-related deaths.

Maybe if it tries real hard, America can catch up with Portugal in terms of evidence-based social policies. I'm doubtful that the Donald will go this route, but then neither did Obama. It's a draw on that one.

THE WAR ON CHILD ABUSE

"Danger, Will Robinson, danger."

"Who? Where from? Muslims? Terrorists? Arabs? People from Yemen, Somalia, Iran, Iraq, Syria, the Sudan and. . . and, I don't know, one other country?"

"No, Will Robinson. Not the Trumped up immigration ban countries. English-speaking Anglo-American Christian fathers, uncles and grandfathers."

"Thank you. Threat identified. Activate strategic threat response systems."

"Roger that, Will Robinson."

Just to review, here are the death counts on US soil in the twenty-first century:

Gun suicides (17 x 18,000)	306,000
Gun homicides (17 x 14,000)	238,000
Child Abuse and Neglect (17 x 1,400)	23,800
Domestic Violence (17 x 1,300)	22,100
9/11	2,977
Trump immigration ban countries	0

Of course, to be scientific, we'd have to break the list of child murder and spousal abuse perpetrators down into White, Hispanic, African-America, Native America, Oriental and so on. The perpetrators aren't all American-born white Christians, but lots of them are. Most of them.

How is the war on child abuse coming along? There isn't one. This is a flaw in our threat analysis. Why do we make this analytical error? Where there's no will, there's no way. It all goes back to Freud. He was the first Pentagon contractor to come up with an effective disinformation strategy for the war on child abuse. In an 1897 letter to his buddy Wilhelm Fleiss, Freud repudiated the seduction theory, which he had previously endorsed due to being foolish and ill-informed.

According to Freud's Seduction Theory, which he endorsed in his 1896 book with Joseph Breuer, entitled Studies on Hysteria, adult women were coming to him for treatment because of symptoms caused by childhood sexual abuse. The sexual abuse, he thought, really happened. But then he changed his mind. In 1897 he repudiated the Seduction Theory and decided that the abuse never happened. It was all false memories, which he called Oedipal fantasies. He created a highly convoluted theory to explain why these women were fantasizing that their fathers had "seduced" them = raped them. These were fantasies that expressed what the little sluts really wanted, which was to be raped by dad.

I'm not kidding, or exaggerating. This was literally Freud's theory. The Jewish fathers in Vienna were very happy to hear that they had never molested their daughters, never, ever. It was all Oedipal fantasies. Thanks Siggy Stardust! Great disinformation strategy. No need for a war on child abuse, because there's no child abuse happening! Problem solved.

"And a jolly good psychiatrist he was, Basil."

"Yes, jolly, jolly good. He is so well loved at the Club."

Freudian theory was swallowed hook, line and sinker by psychiatry. The Boys at the Gentleman's Club applauded and tipped their sherry glasses to Sigmund, all over the world. For most of the twentieth century, psychiatrists knew for a fact that none of these women had actually been abused as children, because incest is very, very rare. No need for a war on child abuse.

Flash forward to 1981. Colin A. Ross, M.D. has just begun his four-year psychiatry residency, not at some pipsqueak place like Yale or Harvard, at the University of Manitoba, in Winnipeg, also affectionately known as Winterpeg. What was the good doctor's textbook for learning everything he needed to know about psychiatry? The Comprehensive Textbook of Psychiatry, 1980 edition. It was really up to date, and contained all the latest and greatest on psychiatry. The text was over 3000 pages.

Way at the back of The Comprehensive Textbook of Psychiatry, 1980 edition, was a section called Topics of Special Interest. This meant, irrelevant rare stuff that we threw in at the back for completeness' sake. Not for the children's sake. In that section there was a short chapter entitled, Incest. In that short chapter on incest there was one paragraph talking about how common incest is in North America. In that short paragraph there was a reference to a 1955 study saying it was one family out of a million in America.

This was official medical, scientific, academic, psychiatric reality in 1980: one family out of a million. It's actually more than one family out of a hundred. Psychiatry was off by a factor of over 10,000. In the DSM-5 this kind of thinking is classified as a delusional disorder. Psychiatry took the lead on male chauvinist pig perpetrator denial of incest throughout the twentieth century. This level of disinformation and cover-up is matched only by the medical profession's battle against accepting that smoking causes lung cancer. This now proven scientific fact was bucked, fought and resisted with the full authority of organized medicine for years, until the pile of evidence became too big to deny any longer. This happened in my lifetime, which places it at least a few years after the Dark Ages.

Medicine, including psychiatry, functioned as the primary social agent for suppressing the reality of childhood sexual abuse throughout the twentieth century. Nice job, colleagues. What brought childhood sexual abuse out of the closet, and along with it physical and verbal abuse, child neglect, spousal battery, date rape and sexual harassment of cute medical students by Professors of Medicine? It wasn't the doctors. It was a bunch of bra-burning, demonstrating, menstruating, marching feminists.

"I say, Basil, which side is this Colin Ross fellow on? Can't he make up his mind? Last we heard from him, he was making fun of the feminazis."

"I know, it's very confusing, Cecil, when it should be all black or all white."

I feel for these British gentlemen, but remember the horseshoe model. The Trump Card is a political satire of extremism at both ends. It's kind of like burning the candle at both ends. Flame on, Avengers!

Without the street fight fought by feminist women who weren't going to take it anymore, I wouldn't have had a career as a specialist in childhood trauma and it's psychological effects. So I can't possibly be against feminism. Nor can I be against psychiatry, since I have been practicing psychiatry since 1985. They say that practice makes perfect, so I'm still at it. I give credit where credit is due and give expulsion products of colonic digestive processes where expulsion products of colonic digestive processes are due. I don't discriminate. This is equal opportunity political satire.

In the twentieth century, psychiatry has grudgingly had to admit that childhood trauma is endemic in America, which is doctor talk for there's a lot of it. But most psychiatrists still don't treat trauma in their practices. Got a symptom? Here, try this pill. See you at your next appointment in six weeks. Have a good day. Don't forget to have sex with your husband whenever he wants it.

We don't have a war on child abuse because we don't want one. At least the Boss Dogs don't. Sure, we acknowledge in theory that it's a big problem, and we throw a few token dollars at it. We have Child Protective Services. We care. Don't complain because the CPS workers are under-trained, overwhelmed with gigantic caseloads, and burned out. We don't have time for that. We're in a War on Terror here. We're up to ours ears in alligators trying to protect the women and children of America from terrorists!

OK, talk, talk, talk. In the end it's all about military contractors and their profits. But we have to sell the taxpayer. We have politicians to do that for us. Listen to them talk, talk, talk about how they're going to protect America! From what? The main threat to America is America. The Islamic jihadists could save themselves a lot of effort. They could just sit back and watch America destroy itself from within. That's where we're headed, with all this polarized partisan bickering and all these verbal drive-by shootings. Allah Bless America!

Oh, I forgot to mention, there's good money in child pornography, under-age prostitution, and sex trafficking. Splash in a little cocaine, and it's a party! Gotta maintain a positive cash flow, man! Or woman. But mostly, man. The women get to be the arm candy, and that's a pretty good deal, but not if they're feminists.

THE WAR ON TERROR

Multiple choice question: why do we have a war on terror? Possible answers: 1) it's a make work project for the military-industrial complex 2) we need the oil 3) we've dicked people in the Middle East around so bad for so long, now we've got to deal with a lot of blowback, 4) all of the above are true. If you answered (4), you could say it's a geopolitical blowjob. Not cocaine, blowback, or maybe on the front, where the big guns are. But no, none of that could be true. We need to get Freud to figure it out for us. He'll find the answer. Finders keepers.

Terminate encrypted transmission. Activate non-encrypted mode.

"Basil, Basil, what is this man talking about?"

"I have no idea."

Sorry for getting distracted there. I remember being a school child in Winnipeg, Manitoba, Canada in 1962. I remember the Cuban Missile Crisis. I remember the Kennedy assassination on November 22, 1963. I remember John Glenn. I remember practicing getting under our school desks as a thermonuclear war drill. We had very sturdy desks.

I remember another drill – we were let out early and walked home from school so that we could join our parents, then everyone in that section of the city would evacuate out Waverley Street in their cars, to safety and survival. Waverley Street was a tree-lined residential thoroughfare that was two lanes wide. All this would take place in an orderly fashion in the five minutes between when the incoming Russian nukes were picked up by the Distant Early Warning radar and when the nuke went kaboom over Winnipeg. The government was taking good care of us. We sure could trust the government.

Also, in this geological era, the government of Canada injected me with viruses that cause cancer in monkeys. This was the SV-40 virus that was present in the monkey kidney cells used in the preparation of the polio vaccine. No biggee! The government was taking care of me. By the way, you might ask, where is the documentation for this absurd conspiracy theory? On the CDC website. Check it out, man, awesome!

I remember Colin Powell enlightening the UN with the fake news that Saddam Hussein had weapons of mass destruction and was responsible for 9/11. You can definitely trust what the government is telling you now. If Trump doesn't have a cozy, trusting relationship with the CIA, that's conclusive evidence that Trump is a nut case, right? Which do you left left left wingers prefer? Two choices here: the cozy Bush/Colin Powell fake news relationship with the CIA, or the Trump I don't buy everything you're saying relationship? Your choice. Your call.

Those who repeat history are doomed to forget it.

So, then, lefters and righters, there is another form of fake news: when the press accurately reports what the White House is saying and we watch videos of Colin Powell's speech at the UN. Now that's real news! But it's fake news because Saddam Hussein had no weapons of mass destruction and no involvement in 9/11.

Speaking of 9/11, everyone knows that Osama bin Laden was behind 9/11. This is an absolute fact, locked down, proven, known for sure. Right? Right. Here is some possibly fake or possibly real news, however: on September 28, 2001, bin Laden denied any involvement in 9/11 in an interview with the Pakistani newspaper, Unmat. The interview was translated and released by the BBC World Monitoring Service on September 29, 2001. Setting aside the possibility that the BBC is a fringe media company that never checks its facts and releases bogus fake news, this is what bin Laden said:

"I have already said that I am not involved in the 11 September attacks in the United States. As a Muslim, I try my best to avoid telling a lie. I had no knowledge of these attacks, nor do I consider the killing of innocent women, children, and other humans as an appreciable act. Islam strictly forbids causing harm to innocent women, children, and other people".

"Such a practice is forbidden ever in the course of a battle. It is the United States, which is perpetrating every maltreatment on women, children, and common people of other faiths, particularly the followers of Islam. All that is going on in Palestine for the last 11 months is sufficient to call the wrath of God upon the United States and Israel."

That's a little weird. Why would bin Laden deny involvement if he was involved? Wouldn't he be more likely to do the opposite, score points with his crew by claiming he was involved when he wasn't? Why did the FBI never indict bin Laden for 9/11 when they did indict him for the embassy bombings in Africa in 1998? Could the reason be that they had no evidence? For that matter, what is the evidence proving that bin Laden was involved in 9/11? I'm not aware of any. If we have some, why would we not release it to the public? Sure, sure, attack me as a conspiracy nut. Fine. Go for it. When you're done, could you show me some actual evidence? Or do you just believe it because Colin Powell said it was so?

The only "evidence" anyone in the trustworthy Government of the United States ever points to is a "confession tape" recovered in a compound in a private home in Jalalabad, Afghanistan, in late November, 2001. Seal Team 6 killed bin Laden on May 2, 2011, nearly 10 years after 9/11, during which time we accumulated zero additional evidence of his involvement in 9/11. If that confession tape is fake, which is a distinct possibility, then we have no actual evidence showing that bin Laden was in fact involved in 9/11. None. Show me some. I mean none. Yet we all know it was him. The only evidence we have is a possibly fake confession tape that is contradicted by bin Laden's statement on September 28, 2001.

The involvement of Osama bin Laden in 9/11 is a shining example of a rush to judgment by the American media and public. The rush occurred in both the Bush and Obama administrations, so it was endorsed by bi-partisan folks, who may be bi themselves, and that's all folks, a bi a bi a bi, or I mean, a be a be a be. That's all folks – and excuthe the thlobber!

SUICIDE BOMBERS: WHAT MAKES THEM TICK?

It's fun writing political satire because you don't have to check your facts. If you make a mistake, you can say it was just a joke. Here's a joke: I was thinking of writing a book with the title, Suicide Bombers. What Makes Them Tick? But – real news, here – I was concerned about getting put on some Middle Eastern hit list. Therefore I thought I would go with just a chapter. By the way, that is not actually the title of this chapter. It's just a typo I didn't catch in proof reading, which I can prove because it was proof reading.

I remember watching an episode of one of those TV cop shows where a cameraman is imbedded in a patrol car and films drug busts and other exciting activities of law enforcement. On this episode, the definitely male voice-over commentator with the hyper-macho voice was telling the viewers what to think and feel while the police chased an apparently drunk driver. It was a pretty slow chase for just a couple of blocks in a neighborhood until the bad guy went over a curb and came to a stop.

Out of the car emerged a very chubby 16-year old boy who started crying and begged the police not to tell his mom. The commentator praised the police for getting another bad guy off the streets, in the same triumphant tone of voice he would use for the capture of a serial killer or a serial bank robber or a heavy-duty drug dealer. This obviously pathetic and disturbed boy was assigned to a new category for life: bad guy felon. He could easily have killed a child, and deserved to be arrested, charged and convicted, but the commentator's attitude, tone and feeling were so ramped up and over-the-top, it was ridiculous. The commentator is lucky that TV hyperbole is not a felony offense.

Same thing with suicide bombers. Evil, evil, evil. The enemy. The bad guys. Again, obviously, suicide bombers should be caught in advance whenever possible, which isn't that often. Not much we can do to them after mission completion. They are mass murderers and if any survive they should at a minimum get life without parole. No doubt about that in my mind. Their support team should get the same sentencing for being co-conspirators. This is true no matter what the race, religion or politics of the suicide bomber. I don't want to hear anything about my being soft on crime or being some kind of bleeding heart liberal on the topic. That said, may I continue?

Let's dissect the terminology. What do we call these people? Suicide bombers. There are two words in that phrase. Taking the second word first, why do we call them suicide bombers? Not hard to figure that out. Because they blow themselves up with bombs. Now the first word. Why do we call them suicide bombers? Because they commit suicide. Hmmmm. . . suicide. I wonder if a psychiatrist might have something to say about that?

This psychiatrist does. First, it seems clear to me that suicide bombers commit suicide. If anybody wants to argue that point, see me out back later. They kill themselves on purpose. This is suicide by any definition. It follows, in my impaired brain, that since suicide bombers commit suicide, then they must have been suicidal before killing themselves. I tried to make this point in a conversation once and got howls of protest, derision and disagreement in response.

If someone gets arrested for drunk driving and has a blood alcohol way above the legal limit, would it be fair to say that the person was driving drunk? If someone commits suicide, would it be fair to say he was suicidal beforehand? If we were talking about everyday American civilian life, there would be nothing to debate. The logic would be self-evident to everyone. So, if someone commits suicide by hanging, he or she was suicidal beforehand. Same for overdose, same for carbon monoxide, same for jumping off a bridge. We don't conclude that a person was not suicidal based on the method of suicide.

So, if an American civilian went out in a field by himself and blew himself up with a bomb, on purpose, we would all agree that he was suicidal. Same thing for a German civilian, or any civilian from any nationality. OK, all agreed so far. So that would include a civilian from Palestine, then. Let's shake on it.

There are many different motives for suicide. Not all people who commit suicide were clinically depressed beforehand – this is accepted as a fact in psychiatry, based on interviews with people before they completed suicide, and interviews with people who intended to die but survived. Everyone still with me?

In my clinical work, I sometimes say that suicide is a murder mystery. The mystery is: who killed who? There are three possible murders: 1) the self killed the self, which is always true 2) the self killed the other, and 3) the other killed the self.

The self killed the other describes the person whose motive is to get revenge on her perpetrators: "You'll be sorry when your daughter is dead." Or, "You'll see what you did to me." Or, "Now you'll feel bad." The person is taking her anger out on herself as a tactic for punishing the people who hurt her.

The other killed the self describes the situation in which the person identifies with, internalizes, and aligns with the perpetrator's anger towards her, and acts the perpetrator's anger out on herself.

The patients in my Trauma Programs are mostly there because they got too suicidal to continue in outpatient treatment. I have explained this scheme to hundreds of suicidal people without any complaints or debates. They see that it is a metaphor designed to help them examine their motives for suicide. Another metaphor I use is that suicide is a coin with two sides. One side I call the euthanasia side. This is suicide for the purpose of ending the pain and suffering – "I'll just ease myself out of here and then everything will be OK. The pain will be over."

I compare the euthanasia side to putting a beloved dog to sleep. The dog is old, blind, arthritic, has cancer, and now is losing control of his bladder and bowels. It is time to take the dog to the vet and have him put to sleep. This is an act of love and kindness. But then there's the other side of the coin: on that side the suicide is an angry, violent hostile murder of a human being. The reason for talking about this side of the coin is that often it is denied or not recognized, but the real energy and drive behind the suicide is self-blame, self-hatred, guilt and anger directed towards the self, in other words, the locus of control shift.

OK, we're agreed then. Suicide bombers kill themselves, which is why we call them suicide bombers. By definition they have to have been suicidal before they killed themselves on purpose in a planned fashion. The motive for the suicide, and the method of suicide, do not alter this basic fact. But already I'm starting to lose some people, who are now going to angrily state that suicide bombers aren't suicidal and we shouldn't feel sorry for them.

At this point, I get it. It's about being tough on crime. If you have any empathy for the criminal, then you're automatically going to give them a soft sentence, which proves you are a bleeding heart liberal. It's all-or-nothing, black-and-white thinking again. In fact, in my mind at least, there is no reason why you can't have empathy with a person but be tough on any crimes he commits. Once you assume that empathy = soft on crime, however, then you have to block any reasons for having empathy. You have to say that suicide bombers aren't suicidal in order not to go boo hoo hoo. The right wing is afraid you're going to tell suicide bombers to have a nice day.

What if trying to understand the psychology of suicide bombers was part of planning the war on terror? As far as I know, no senior military person has ever claimed that the war on terror can be won solely by military means. This should be a given in any planning. Diplomacy, sanctions, negotiations, financial aid and a host of other strategies should be considered. One of these might be understanding the psychology of why young people in the Middle East blow themselves up.

Clearly, suicide bombers are driven by numerous different financial, cultural, religious, political and other forces. No one factor can account for everything, and neither can any one academic discipline. I'm not saying that we should regard suicide bombers as mentally ill or try to make DSM-5 diagnoses on them, both of which would be a waste of time. Suicide bombers: what makes them tick?

I remember reading about a young Palestinian suicide bomber who was wrestled to the ground and disarmed in Israel. During his interrogation, he spouted the standard rhetoric about the crimes of the Israeli state and how all Israelis are complicit and responsible for the crimes of their state, therefore they are all enemy combatants, and therefore it is a legitimate act of war to bomb Israeli citizens, along with oneself. I'd summarize this as blah, blah, blah, blah.

At this point the interrogator could have hooded the young Palestinian, water boarded him, insulted the Koran, had a female officer come in and humiliate him sexually, staged a mock dog attack, or used any other manner of enhanced interrogation tactics. Instead, the interrogator started talking to the suicide bomber about football (no, not the NFL, soccer). The bomber, it turned out, was an enthusiastic football fan and knew every player on the Israeli football team. After talking about football for a while, the interrogator asked the bomber what he would do if his handlers told him to go to a football match and blow up the Israeli soccer team.

How did the bad guy respond? He said there is no way he would do that. What was the interrogation technique? To humanize the targets of the bombing. Obviously, this would take a lot of conversations, a lot, one might say, of therapy. The bomber would still have to stand trial and serve his sentence, but now we would have some information of potential future strategic and tactical use. The way to disarm the bombers is to humanize their targets. This can't be done with hate literature or rants about Islamic terrorism. It's a strategy for disarming the enemy, not for being soft on him. In order to do this, we have to humanize the targets of our interrogations.

The people in terrorist videos are like cartoon characters and their targets are cartoon characters to them. It's not a funny Saturday morning cartoon, but the terrorists are in costumes, with masks, and there is clearly a cultural script being followed. This is all understandable – it's what a young single guy has to do in the Middle East in order to get laid. I bet those 70 virgins in Heaven can hardly wait till he arrives!

Is it possible that the suicide bombers have been tricked and exploited by their leaders? We don't seem to see any 50-year old terrorists volunteering as suicide bombers. Could it be that the suicide bombers are victims of enhanced interrogations done on them by their handlers? The techniques of the Islamic terrorist brainwashing are a little different, but brainwashing it is. If we hate the suicide bombers, we are just providing them a portrait that justifies their attacks on us. They look in the mirror and see us. They kill the enemy without in order to kill the enemy within.

In the book version of Suicide Bombers. What Makes Them Tick?, one of the chapters was entitled, "Too Much Dust, Not Enough Sex." That pretty well summarizes the problem, in my opinion.

Post-summary: To post-summarize, the psychodynamics of suicide that I talk about with my patients could be applied to the war on terror. In terms of the murder mystery, suicide bombing is an example of the self killed the other. The suicide bomber kills the self in order to harm the other (us). This is literally true. To kill his target, the bomber must dehumanize his target. Calling the target a target and the bystanders collateral damage helps with the process. But he must also dehumanize himself. I imagine that the locus of control shift must be operating in the suicide bomber: I am disposable, my family will be better off if I'm dead (which is literally true financially due to payments to the martyr's family), and what I'm doing is justified (by my suffering or by geopolitics).

Can we agree that no one who feels good about himself commits suicide? The psychological mechanism of projection must also be involved: I will project my bad self onto the enemy and kill him. Talk about war games! We demonize them, they demonize us, we demonize their demonization of us, we quote the bible, they quote the Koran, and on and on it goes. The war on terror is an endless Fight Club combat ritual with oneself, conducted in a parking lot called Planet Earth. This is why US drone pilots refer to their targets as bug splatter. It's a dehumanized video game. These days, we train our children for this psychology starting at a very early age, desensitizing them through violent video games.

Hey, it's just a game!

A PSYCHOLOGICAL PROFILE OF OSAMA BIN LADEN

I published a psychological profile of Osama bin Laden in the Journal of Psychohistory, referenced below. I made two main points in that paper: I tried to humanize bin Laden and I pointed out that, as Philip Seymour Hoffman's character said in the movie, Charlie Wilson's War, "We f'ed up the end game." I'll repeat those two points here and embellish them a little.

First, the end game. We use people as disposable pawns in our geopolitical chess game all the time. Saddam Hussein, check. Manuel Noriega, check. Osama bin Laden, check. Dozens of other leaders of sundry inconsequential banana republics over the last seventy years, check. But no check mate. It's a Mad Hatter's Tea Party game that goes on forever. If not forever, at least for thousands of years. The two main branches of Islam are killing each other today because of an unresolved dispute between Mohammed's relatives in the seventh century, plus a few contemporary power struggles added in. But we're going to win this war real quick, says Trump.

Shortly after 9/11, I was in a restroom in Michigan using the urinal. As I looked down, I was both amused and alarmed to see a plastic photo of Osama bin Laden in each urinal. I was literally pissing on the most evil terrorist in the world. Does it seem odd that we knew for sure it was bin Laden within a couple of days of 9/11? Everyone knew this for a fact almost immediately, but ten years later the FBI had still not presented any actual conclusive evidence to the public. You have to trust the Government.

We had bin Laden demonized and convicted almost immediately after 9/11, without any evidence. That's called American Justice. Guilty without a trial. Hang 'em high! And meanwhile, the American grannies knitted sweaters for their grand-children while watching and applauding. We were completely justified in convicting bin Laden based solely on rumors reported by our trustworthy, non-fake-news media because we sure as Hell needed someone to blame. As usual, it was a lone gunman, this time with a few accomplices.

If we had our hands on bin Laden, we would have executed him on the spot, just like we did in the compound in Abuttisbad, Pakistan, or however you spell it. There is no way an entire Seal team could have taken him alive. What, you think the US military has incapacitants? That's science fiction. We respect Islam so much that we wage war against Islamic terrorism and block Muslims from seven different countries from coming into the US, and that's why we buried Osama bin Laden at sea so no one could see the body, because we really respect him and his religion, and we didn't want to rile up al Qaeda by killing its leader, but we had to because he hit us first and so we had to hit him back because that's how adults handle things, so get that straight and if you disagree with me you can damn well go to your room without any dinner.

I'm confused on one point. Help me out here. Is it really true that we used to lynch Negroes without a trial in the United States of America? Did that really occur numerous times within my parents' lifetimes? Really? You're not kidding me? Good old Americano Gringos lynching people without a trial? No way. That would never happen. And if it did happen, we stopped that a long time ago because now we're loving inclusive folks and we love Bernie and Hillary and each other and everybody. Group hug! Group hug! But not you, Osama bin. We lynched you without a trial, which was damn well justified because we're white and you're black, or at least light black. Too much melanin in your skin, anyway, for sure. And we know that was righteous because we saw that photo of Hillary watching the Abuttisbad raid with her honest American friends, who are nothing like George Bush and his Evil Gang, who almost deserve lynching too, because he was never Our President of Our Country, that's for sure.

It's our God-given duty to fight Satan wherever we see him, such as inside Donald Trump, where he is having quite the party these days. He's trying to interfere with us bringing in illegal Mexicans to do jobs that are too much work for us at pay we'd never accept, and that's sure a human rights violation by the Donald, that's for sure, and we're sure about it, sure as shootin', I know for sure.

Well, what about Osama bin? Fact: we funded the resistance against the Russians when their Evil Empire was occupying Afghanistan, also known as Afgunistan. We poured in some billions to that righteous war, which was righteous because Russia is Evil and we are Good, in case you didn't know. And who was one of the top dogs in the Holy Resistance to Evil Russia that we were fighting with our hearts and souls and later on with our Apache helicopters? Osama bin. He was our man in Afgunistan. Technically, he was a CIA asset, which is why we later kicked his ass.

What happened when our Holy Asset won our Holy War for us? We dropped him. We worked with our allies, the good people of Saudi Arabia, who only stone women to death when they deserve it, aka, hurt the bitch, to help them remove Osama bin's passport and exile him to some country in Africa where we later had a small Blackhawk Down problem. We blocked him from organizing the Mujahideen to fight against Saddam Hussein; we screwed him over royally, with help from the Saudi royals, who sure have lots of oil. Surprisingly, this made him a little bit ticked off the US of A. Tick, tick, tick. What made Osama bin Laden tick?

If bin Laden was behind 9/11, then 9/11 was a classical example of blowback. It likely could have been prevented by honoring him, thanking him for his service, and treating him decently after he was discharged from our deniable Army. But we don't even treat American veterans decently, so why should we treat our assets in the Middle East decently after we don't need their asses anymore, the stupid assets? We talk the talk about honoring the troops, but we give them pathetic levels of support, most of the time, in terms of access to

VA treatment that is actually helpful and actually lasts longer than a couple of sessions followed by a slap on the back and preceded by months on a waiting list. That's how we treat people on our team, so it's bad news for people on the opposing team.

How did it feel to be an African-American in the US in the 1950's? Ask a Muslim in the US today. Those who repeat history are doomed to forget it.

Did you know that Osama bin Laden was basically an orphan? His mother was one of his father's many wives, but the wives were ranked in a very rigid hierarchy, and she was way down the totem pole. Osama was one of over 50 children. He didn't get to live in the main compound with his father, and was banished to another domicile 50 miles away. His higher-ranking siblings mocked him mercilessly for this. In case you've never heard the term, this is called childhood trauma. Oh, whoops, sorry, there I go feeling empathy with black people again.

There was only one arena in which young Osama excelled, got to spend time with his father, and rose to the top of the hierarchy. This was when he spent two weeks every year camping out in the desert with his father and brothers, hunting and riding camels. Lock that into the psyche for future reference.

As a teenager and young man, Osama was quite the party animal. In school in Beirut he had a handle bar moustache, his own table at local bars, consorted with ladies of the night, got into bar fights, and tooled around in a cool Mercedes. Also, he wore bell-bottomed trousers. Check out the photos of him on a Christmas ski vacation with his Christian girlfriend and her family! I don't know for sure, but I'm thinking that family was likely in the top 1%, as was Osama bin as an adult, when his net worth was in the hundreds of millions.

Things got dicey in Beirut due to some geopolitical chess moves and bombs going off, so his family pulled him back to Saudi Arabia to protect him from the Muslim violence going on in Beirut. Osama toned it down a bit back home due to being under closer surveillance, which Muslims have to do to Muslims to keep them in line, but he still tooled around in a yellow Mercedes for a while. His up-the-totem-pole siblings tried to convert him to orthodox, observant Islam but were unsuccessful for a while, until Osama bin had a religious conversion. Then he swung from black to white. He out-fundamentalized his siblings, which hopefully scored him points with his devoutly religious mega-wealthy construction contractor father, who also brought top religious scholars to his home for encounter groups, except he didn't call them encounter groups.

Through a series of steps, Osama was dumped, ostracized by the Saudi Royal family, rejected by his own family, had his Saudi passport revoked, and somehow, by some mysterious process, ended up getting radicalized. Who knows how?

How could Osama bin ever get back into the good graces of his father on earth and His Father in Heaven? How about a holy jihad against the infidels who are disrespecting the Holy Sites of Mecca and Medina and stationing their troops in the Holy Land (Saudi Arabia, not Israel) in order to fight their old asset, now their Evil Enemy Saddam Hussein instead of using their old asset Osama bin and his Band of Merry Men to fight Saddam and his Evil Sons? Somebody in this story is evil, and it sure ain't us, says the United States of America, Praise the Lord. Somebody in this story is evil, and it sure ain't us, says al Qaeda, Praise Allah.

Here's a pagan idea for you: maybe we are all God's children. Maybe he loves us all. Or no, what am I talking about? That doesn't make any sense. Nuke them terrorists, man! And boy, do those defense contractors have some sweet health insurance policies! Their health premiums are included as expenses in their defense contracts, at least for the ones who know how to negotiate. It's called The Art of the Deal. There are always winners and losers in the game of life. It's the law of the jungle. The only way to escape that jungle is to go back to the land and live a righteous life close to God, which in the Middle East means caves in Tora Bora. It's all a plan to recapture that feeling of camping with your dad in the desert.

Who was that other guy who went out in the desert for a long time? Forty days and forty nights, I think it was.

Ross, C.A. (2015). A psychological profile of Osama bin Laden. Journal of Psychohistory, 42, 4, 310-319.

A PSYCHOLOGICAL PROFILE OF ELIAN GONZALEZ

Since I had nothing better to do with my time, I also published a psychological profile of Elian Gonzalez in the Journal of Psychohistory, referenced below. Elian was a regular kid who happened to be born in Cuba, which was ruled over by an Evil Communist Tyrant named Fidel Castro. We were able to invade Panama and depose its leader and we invaded Iraq and deposed its leader and we tried hard to depose Fidel but Cuba was just too big and advanced and armed and tough and stuff like that for us ever to depose Fidel, but we sure tried our best, you can believe that if you want.

While we were trying hard to depose Fidel we also used a little corner of his island as a military base called Guantanamo Bay, but we didn't talk much about how that deal was set up or what the annual rent was, if there was any rent. We just didn't have the military resources to take over the whole island but we should have, to help spread freedom and democracy and Good.

Once upon a time there was another little kid named Omar Khadr who was a Canadian citizen but he was in his kinda home country in the Middle East, Afgunistan if I remember right, when a platoon of US soldiers marched up to his small town, which resulted in a fire fight starting, through no fault of the US soldiers. These Afgunistaners had the gall to try to protect themselves when a bunch of foreigners marched into their village. Omar was twelve at the time. During the fire fight, supposedly, Omar threw a grenade, although the eye witness testimony by the American troops afterwards was conflicted and it isn't certain he ever did throw a grenade, but if he did that sure took a lot of nerve and he sure deserved to get his butt whipped, which he did. We tried him as a war criminal for getting himself injured in a firefight we started when he was 12 and maybe for trying to fight back, but we're not 100% sure about that part.

Omar was found badly injured under a pile of rubble and captured and transported to a secure location, and then he got lucky and won an extended vacation at Guantanamo Bay when he was 15, at which time he was a child who should have come under the protection of Child Protective Services since he was on God-fearing US soil. But he didn't. Instead he was subjected to enhanced interrogations. This means that, as a child, Omar Khadr was systematically abused by the US government on US soil, which would be a criminal offense if it was done by civilians. You have to trust the Government.

I just wanted to get things clear. The Good US tortured a child in Cuba and Fidel Castro was Evil. Why did we torture Omar Khadr? Because, we claim, his father had contact with Osama bin Laden. This made Omar a high value target at age 12 because you can be sure that the terrorist network that hid Osama bin from the US military, the CIA and the NSA for 10 years after 9/11 had really lax security protocols in place and definitely could have told a 12-year old kid their state secrets, which we had to try to pry out of him for National Security reasons so we could find Osama bin and chat with him, which explains why we continued to keep Omar at Guantanamo By after we had respectfully buried Osama bin at sea in 2015, or 2011, or whatever year it was. Hard to remember since the bin Laden raid happened so far back in history.

Back to that other kid, Elian. His parents divorced, trauma number one, and his Good Mother decided to kidnap him and take him away from his father to Good America. There was never any allegation of abuse or bad parenting by Elian's father. Elian's Good Mother took him on a raft or a boat or some kind of vessel that is very safe for children and left for Good America, except the vessel was so unsafe and the crew and conditions so bad that they capsized and the Good Mom drowned, which was certainly a good trauma to put Elian through, and incidentally is conclusive proof that God was on her side.

Elian floated around on vacation in a life vest or an inner tube or some other high-tech safety device approved for the use of children in shark-infested waters for a few days until some fishermen found him and brought him to Good America. Thankfully, God's plan was realized, and Elian was put in the care of his relatives in Miami, who he had never met. For some reason, though, the Evil Government of Cuba and Elian's Evil Father objected to Elian being kidnapped and taken out of the country without the father's permission, without any legal process, and without any independent party ascertaining what Elian wanted. This is typical for Cubans, who don't know what real freedom and democracy are all about.

After a bunch of high-level diplomatic doing-nothing (aka, business as usual in Washington), the INS decided that Elian had to be kidnapped by the US Government. Rather than discussing this rationally like a bunch of infants, the INS instead raided the relatives' home at gunpoint in full tactical gear with automatic weapons and other toys designed for the welfare of children. The picture of Elian overwhelmed with terror while the Good Guys were kidnapping him at gunpoint was in the news all over the world. Trauma number three.

What did the Good US end up doing? Because we believe in freedom and democracy and because we know that Communism is bad, bad, bad, we sent Elian back to Cuba to be with his father. That make sense? If you think it makes sense for the Government of the United States to raid a home at gunpoint in order to capture a child and extradite him to a Communist country, please explain it to me. Elian wasn't even a Muslim.

After we returned Elian Gonzalez to his father in Cuba, we were able to keep Guantanamo Bay, which is good because where else would a Good Country be able to incarcerate and torture a 15-year old boy with no legal consequences? That would be hard to do in Iowa or New Hampshire and besides, doing that on US soil might get the bleeding heart liberals who don't believe in torturing children all riled up, and we sure don't want that because the primaries are pretty important in a free democracy.

Thank you, Good Obama, for keeping the world safe by imprisoning Omar Khadr at Guantanamo Bay. We love you. We hate Trump. Oh, and thanks for not closing Guantanamo Bay like you promised you would, because we sure need a place we can torture people out of sight and out of mind so we can keep on loving you and hating Trump and not being confused about anything.

Ross, C.A. (2014). A psychological profile of Elian Gonzalez. Journal of Psychohistory, 41, 276-282.

MELANIA: TOO HOT FOR THE WHITE HOUSE

Did you know that Donald Trump is a xenophobe racist? Yeah, he hates immigrants. Even married one. I rest my case. I think I'll just leave my case on the floor while I watch some football, since I just have to reach down into my cooler, which I conveniently have placed by the couch, so that I could put my case of beer in it. It's a cold case, but let's talk about it anyway, before the case turns hot, or at least warm, which can happen when there are two football games in a row.

Speaking of hot, not cold cases, Melania Trump is definitely hot – the evidence being those modeling photos of her, like the one in the slightly kinky metal bikini or whatever that not-100%-Christian garment was. No wonder the feminists hate her. If she would just dress like a librarian from outer space and maybe burn a bra or two, or at least a bikini, maybe she would be tolerable. But to have a successful daughter who is also very attractive – heresy! What is America coming to? Ivanka and Melania – it's just too much for the feminists!

Whoops. I'm getting confused again. If Hillary had won, then Bill would have become the First Husband. Imagine how Saturday Night Live would have milked that one! Whoops. I'm getting confused again. No one makes fun of Eleanor Roosevelt or Betty Ford. They weren't too hot for their own good, that's why. Well, maybe not for their own good, but definitely for the good of feminists everywhere. It's much more righteous to be plain, even dowdy, and you sure shouldn't dress up to please men like some bimbo. No, you should wear the outfits prescribed by the business world if you want to move up in corporate America. Equal pay for equal work, I say, but not equal dress codes for Melania and Hillary. Hillary knows the rules.

Bill knows the rules too. That's why he had to have so many affairs: one dress code for the wife, one for the mistress. And that's the trouble with Melania Trump – she dresses and looks like the mistress, but she's the wife. Very confusing, for feminists and male chauvinist pigs, who don't get why their wives look like Hillary. Could have something to do with your net worth, boys.

It's one crazy world out there, that's for sure. Now we have a bimbo for first lady who only speaks four or five languages fluently, not like all those other Appropriate Role Model First Ladies, who only spoke one. Fortunately, they spoke American, which is the only language that counts, and without an accent. And yes, we're very inclusive, but only of everyone who agrees with us and plays by our rules. If you don't, then we reject you totally, like totally, man.

TRUMP'S HOUSE AND SADDAM HUSSEIN'S PALACE

I think Donald Trump and Saddam Hussein used the same interior decorator. Lots of gold, huge rooms with high ceilings, expensive antique furniture; I'll go for broke and guess that the style might be called Baroque, if not Byzantine, or Bankrupt. Definitely not Gothic. Come to think of it, not Bankrupt either. One of these men is the President of the United States and the other was an Evil Dictator. The far left wing of the US political spectrum thinks the Donald is, or is about to become, an Evil Dictator. That would make sense, since he has Evil Decorator tastes in interior design and wives, and probably drinks expensive wine, which he pays for out of the money he made as an American entrepreneur in the Land of Opportunity, which seems to be against American values according to the left wing of the chicken, which can't even fly because its left wing and its right wing can't work together. But that chicken sure can cluck!

What did we do when we liberated Iraq from an evil dictatorship and toppled Saddam's statue and killed only a few hundred thousand Iraqi civilians with shock and awe bombing runs, sanctions, and other tools of democracy? We didn't behave like those ISIS barbarians who are destroying ancient architecture in the Middle East. No, siree! We looted Evil Saddam's palace, that's what we did, because we're Good and we took some good photos of US troops sitting on Saddam's gold toilets. I bet we even pissed on his floors like we pissed on Osama bin Laden's face in urinals in Michigan after 9/11.

I feel sorry for heterosexual American women – they have to date American men, of which epidemiological sample, approximately 95% are developmentally arrested in early adolescence, with a thin veneer of adulthood laid on top. You have to have that veneer in order to get laid in America, once you're over thirty, or a lot of money, which, as we know, is an aphrodisiac surpassed by no other, at least among American women, who naturally need decent jewelry and breast implants and want to send their kids to the most expensive private schools so they can be better than everyone else they're equal to, which we teach in church in America.

THE KENNEDY MAFIA WAS GOOD, THE TRUMP MAFIA IS BAD

The Kennedys – now there's a political mafia. A brother in the White house, another one in the Senate, and another one the Attorney General. We call that Camelot, not Camel-A-Lot, which they do in the Middle East. We revere and idolize JFK and his kin. Gorgeous family photos in the White House and at Hyannis Port. Photos out sailing, wind in the hair, Jack playing with the children, then John Jr. saluting to his father's casket.

Well, at least some of us revere Camelot, but not the Texas oilmen, and not the military contractors. John and Bobby were planning on pulling the troops out of Vietnam, which would have been very bad for the defense contractors. On top of that, according to the right wing, JFK was soft on Castro, which was bad for the Mafia gambling interests. And on top of that mountain of extruded end products of intestinal digestion, the brothers re-districted. The right wing does this, but only for righteous reasons to help America. The Kennedy brothers analyzed the 1960 Presidential voting in every district in the USA to determine which districts that voted Republican had which military contractors, and they planned to shift the contracts to states that voted Democrat, in an effort to re-secure the White House next time around. This is not the way business gets done in America.

I'm not building up to a theory about who killed JFK or why. I'm just pointing out that while most of America was idealizing Camelot, the far right wing was devaluing it. This was happening because the country as a whole has borderline personality disorder.

Then we had Bushalot. One father the President, then a son the President and meanwhile another upstart son the Governor of Florida. No wind in the hair for the Bush mafia. They were the Evil Empire, run by Darth Bush on behalf of the Illuminati, at least according to the extreme left wing. There's a Bush behind every bush.

Thankfully, we got rid of the Bushes while preserving the environment. Then we had Obama-a-lot. Wind in the hair again, except for Barack, whose hair is not that dreamy. Michelle and helping school children. Beautiful daughters who never got caught doing anything wrong. But sadly, the Obamalots had to move out.

In come the Trumpalots, who we know are evil because the Donald redecorated a little just like every President before him. When he redecorates it's evil, unlike when Jackie redecorated, which was another wind in the hair moment. Jackie was pretty and elegant, but not hot. The attractive Trumpalot children are just a bunch of narcissistic Papa yes men and women. Not like Jackie, who never looked the other way and never stood by her man through countless affairs the way Hillary did.

While we're at it, let's demonize President Trump as a womanizer. But not Bill and Jack. No, they get a free pass because we believe in equality and equal pay for equal work and being inclusive and peanut butter and jelly sandwiches and apple pie and Democrats and American stuff like that. No wind in the hair at the White House on Thanksgiving in 2017, I don't think.

A CRAZY LITTLE THING CALLED THE DEFENSE AUTHORIZATION ACT

The military budget gets budged every year through the Defense Authorization Act. One year, that sly Barack guy slipped a little piece of legislation into the Defense Authorization Act, which he did so that the evil Republicans didn't notice it and block it. We don't live in a fascist state because we have voting and freedom and democracy and stuff like that. Only a right wing conspiracy theorist would call Barack a left wing fascist. We know different. Barack good. Donald bad. It's all clear in our minds.

What little, tiny, small, nano-sized, almost invisible authority did the Good Barack slip into law without anyone noticing but a few right wing nut jobs? Just a little boost to the power of the Executive Branch, without any pesky checks or balances from the Judicious Branch or that other unnecessary branch that does legislation. It was no big deal. It was just a little adjustment so that Good Barack could better protect us from terrorists.

Thanks to Barack Obama, I'm pleased to announce, we now live in a country in which the President can order the execution of any individual on the planet, including any American citizen, in any country in the world, at any time. He can do so with legal impunity, with no legal process, and with no oversight from the Legislative Branch, who just get in the way anyway. He can authorize and order the US military to carry out the execution.

President Obama maintained a kill list for the War on Terror Video Game. One of his targets was an American citizen in Yemen, one Anwar al-Awlaki, who had been an imam in the US, and who had contact with 3 of the 9/11 hijackers and Nidal Hasan, the Fort Hood shooter. He had not been charged with any crime on US soil, had not gone through any American legal process, and had not appeared in any American court, but he was regarded as a key figure in the recruitment and radicalization of Arab Muslim men. For the sake of discussion, let's agree that he was one bad dude. Maybe as bad as black drive-by shooters and gang members in New York, LA and Chicago, who nevertheless have a right to due process.

On September 30, 2011, al-Awlaki was killed by a drone strike ordered by President Obama as a targeted execution. Problem solved. A round of self-congratulations, back-slapping and high fives, and we can all have a good night's rest. Two weeks later, Anwar's 16-year old son, Abdulrahmin al-Awlaki, was killed by an Obama-ordered drone strike. More bug splatter. Collateral damage.

This is what the Good Obama does. He respects Muslims and won the Nobel Prize and is inclusive and gives group hugs to liberals. What does the Evil Trump do? Well, he's completely different. We know that. On January 29, 2017,

Nawar al-Awlaki, Anwar's 8-year old daughter, was killed during a commando raid ordered by President Trump. More bug splatter. More collateral damage. You have to cut off the head of the snake, and then you have to cut off the heads of the snake's children too, it seems.

I've reviewed these facts in order to prove that Obama is Good and Trump is Bad. That's easy to see – just look at the Trump Card. It's all right there. Then look at the Obama card – a completely different picture there. Note that I am not commenting on foreign policy or the strategic necessity of the al-Awlaki operations. I'm talking about the ridiculous, uninformed, ahistorical idealization of Obama and devaluation of Trump by the left wing. Ridiculous. Boys and girls, how are you enjoying your Kool-Aid?

THE PATRIOT ACT: GOD BLESS AMERICA

Back in the Dark Ages before the Era of Obama, aka, the Enlightenment, George Bush signed into law a piece of legislation called The Patriot Act. Notice that he didn't call it The Totalitarian State Act. That doesn't have quite the same ring to it. What powers does the Patriot Act give the Government of the United States? The Government can order the detention of any US citizen at any time with no legal charges being filed. The detainee has no right to any legal process including no right to have a lawyer. He can be held indefinitely, literally for years or decades with no charges being filed.

This is called fascism, in case you don't have a dictionary handy. This is a Police State. But sleep little baby, don't you cry, daddy will sing you a lullaby. These two pieces of legislation, the Patriot Act and the clause in the NDAA authorize the Dictator of the United States to order the murder or life imprisonment of any American citizen at any time, including on Sundays, because God rests on Sundays but the White House doesn't. The lullaby is called the War on Terror. Or maybe it's not a lullaby, maybe it's an opiate. Perhaps the DEA or the CDC or one of those other trustworthy arms of the US government could tell us which it is. Huh, I wonder how the right wing militia in America gets radicalized?

This legislation can all be explained by the evil nature of Republicans. But wait a minute, it's Obama who empowered the President of the United States to order the extra-judicial execution of anyone anywhere. Technically, this is called Summary Execution. And I didn't notice Obama repealing the Patriot Act anytime in his eight years, but they went by awfully fast and he was really busy, so that explains that. I'm not holding my breath waiting for Trump to repeal either of those pieces of legislation.

But don't worry. You can trust the Government. We're here to protect the American people. There are all kinds of threats against you by the Bad People. We need these powers of summary execution and extra-judicial imprisonment to protect you from the Bad People, especially in an emergency. We would never use those powers on you because we belong to the Boy Scouts of America. You can trust us. As you know, absolute power never corrupts anyone, not even the people who give themselves absolute power.

WE DON'T DO THAT: WE'RE THE BOY SCOUTS OF AMERICA

Oh, never mind, I covered that in the previous chapter. You can sell the populace anything once you sell them the Boy Scouts Lie.

I remember watching a documentary about military operations in Iraq. A very tough career Sergeant – or maybe a slightly higher rank – was being interviewed in a desert landscape. The documentary included combat scenes and bullets bouncing off of US equipment, but none of the footage was shot up close. The officer was explaining that the military had Iraq divided up into sectors on a grid. His responsibility was to clear the enemy out of a particular grid sector, which he felt he had done pretty well, despite the fact that he and his men were still taking fire.

The interviewer asked him what was happening in the next grid sector over. The officer said that no progress had been made there, but in any case that sector wasn't his responsibility. The interviewer asked the officer if he thought all the stress and combat and loss of American lives was worth it.

This tough, tough stone-faced soldier almost broke down and started crying, before he said, "I have to believe that."

We have to be the Boy Scouts. That has to be true, has to, has to, has to, otherwise we couldn't handle the truth, just like Jack Nicklaus said to Tom Cruise.

WHY I EMIGRATED TO THE UNITED STATES

The United States is the greatest country in the world. No question in my mind. I didn't move to the US and take out citizenship because I don't like America. I emigrated to the United States for several reasons: 1) better weather 2) a better economy and lower taxes 3) a better airport and easier, cheaper domestic air travel 4) much, much better career opportunities, including much more opportunity for entrepreneurship. I have Trauma Programs at three different hospitals – this couldn't happen in any other English-speaking country in the world. Overall, life is much better for me in the United States than in Canada.

What do I like about Canada? The environment. The lack of such a large extreme right wing faction compared to the US. I grew up in Canada and have friends and family there. I remember an event at a Toronto Maple Leafs hockey game a few years back, that I caught online. A Canadian woman was brought out onto the ice on a red carpet, where she was surprised by her partner, who had returned from deployment. The couple kissed and the crowd gave a big cheer. This would never happen at a Dallas Stars game, either the event or the crowd reaction. Why? Because it was a lesbian couple.

What do I not like about Canada, besides the winters? I remember talking with the Trauma Program Director in Dallas a year or two after I arrived in 1991. Her father, who lived in the US, was about the same age as a man I knew in Canada. Both were diagnosed with abdominal aortic aneurysms in the same week, and both sets of doctors thought surgery was required because of the sizes of the aneurysms. When an abdominal aneurysm ruptures, it's instant death. The man in the US had surgery the next week. The man in Canada was put on a 9-month waiting list.

Canada is crippled by bureaucracy and it stifles entrepreneurship compared to the United States. People ask me which country has a better health care system. I always give the same answer: 1) both systems are highly dysfunctional, and 2) you can't give an overall answer – it depends where you are in the economy. If you are in top quarter of the economy, you are better off in the US because you can get quick access to high quality care and can actually afford it. If you're in the bottom quarter of the economy, you're better off in Canada because you have free access to the same care as everyone else gets. If there is a real emergency in Canada, the system gets you in. The bottlenecks are for chronic care.

In the US, my health care costs me less in premiums than the amount I save in taxes; personal income, federal and sales taxes combined. So my not-free US health care is actually freer for me than my Canadian health care was. I can't convince Canadians that they do not in fact have free health care, however. They can't grasp the concept that it's not really free because they have to pay exorbitant taxes to get it. So, for me, health care is better in America.

I remember being at a youth Olympiad in north-central Italy prior to 9/11. The all-star basketball team was playing a select Italian team. The final score was 152-35. The US out-performs Canada in every major sport except ice hockey. I like that about the US, the competitive spirit, the be all you can be attitude. When I compare US film and television to Canada. . . well, never mind. There is a huge variety in US cities and landscapes compared to Canada, especially if we remember to include Hawaii and Alaska, and they are much more accessible. It would cost me more to fly to northern Canada, where I used to live, than to Europe. Domestic airfare in Canada is ridiculously expensive and you're getting nailed with some tax every time you turn around there.

Texas has no state income tax, consequently it sucks horribly on social services. But for me, personally, that works to my advantage. I know, I know, that makes me a bad person. Could we agree that I, personally, don't make the laws? Never mind, it's hopeless – me liking what works for me is indecent and against democracy. I get it. White privilege. Blah, blah, blah.

Is America perfect? Not quite. But it is wonderful. It is a land of contrasts – a great military, great entertainment industry, great space program (at least compared to Canada), but a horrible murder rate and endemic racism. America is such a bundle of contrasts and contradictions. As an American citizen, I reserve the right to free speech and the right to criticize the right, plus the left to criticize the left.

Oh, geez, I just realized I forgot to give instructions on how to read this book. If you are on the left, applaud when I attack the right and ignore the rest. If you are on the right, applaud when I attack the left and ignore the rest. That will save you a lot of time and postage costs, because you won't have to send me any hate mail.

DRONE STRIKES: THE OBAMA CARD

Once again, can we all agree that Trump is Evil, even worse than George Bush? Good. Now let's look at the evidence. Skynet is up and operational in the United States of America, thanks to the good work at Cyberdyne. We live in a total surveillance state. No need to worry, though, because there's always something to watch on TV.

"Terminator, terminator, what do you see?"

"I see an Obama Card looking at me."

We can't trust anything the Governator says, because he's a Republican. But nevertheless, let's talk about drones, droids, cyborgs, computer systems and other tools of the Democratic party. Let's look at drone strikes under Obama, remembering that Obama loves Muslims a lot more than George Bush ever did, or Donald Trump ever will. Don't get confused by the fact that Trump actually talked to Muslims, did business with them, and thereby helped their economies. That doesn't count. No points scored there.

How many drone strikes did the US throw at the Muslim world during the Bush administration, and how many during the Obama administration? Well, it looks like Obama ordered more drone strikes in the first year of his Presidency than Bush did during his entire 8 years: a total of 563 strikes, most of them by drones, under 8 years of Obama compared to 57 under 8 years of Bush. The estimate of civilian drone casualties during the Obama administration runs between 384 and 807, depending on the source of the estimate.

What were the countries targeted with drone strikes by Obama? Pakistan, Somalia and Yemen. Say what? Two of those countries are on the temporary Trump immigration ban. A temporary immigration ban is called a diplomatic strategy. So when Trump uses a diplomatic strategy to exert pressure on the countries supplying ISIS, we call that racism, Islamophobia, and whatever other pooh pooh names we can think of. When Obama uses drone strikes that kill hundreds of civilians, we prefer that, apparently, at least on the left. The right wing, on the other hand, has an equally confusing problem: how can Obama be more of a bad ass than George Bush? The solution on both sides is not to think about it too much.

Imagine life as a civilian in Yemen. A drone could hit you at any time. If not a drone, a smart bomb controlled by a satellite. Imagine the terror we are creating with our war to end terror. Maybe drone strikes are more the problem than the solution.

Anyway, after the outrage has settled down, what is so horrible about a 90-day immigration ban? The word for that is temporary. I waited years to get my green card – a 90-day delay is peanuts compared to my experience. Ninety days at the beginning of an administration to review procedures and make any necessary adjustments. That's a human rights violation? I call it a fast track.

In 1989, I applied to the Government of Manitoba for funding for one research nurse position. During the previous four years since completing my residency in 1985, I had published more papers, obtained more drug company contracts, published more books (one), and obtained more research grant dollars than all the other 100 psychiatrists in the Province of Manitoba combined. By the time I left in 1991, my application hadn't yet made it through the committee structure at the hospital, and hadn't yet been received by the Provincial Government, where it would have to go through more layers of committees. When I talked to the Director of Nursing in the Department of Psychiatry at St. Boniface Hospital, where I worked, in 1991, she estimated that it would be two more years before I heard anything from the Government, and the answer would be 'no.'

It's a little bit of a stretch for me to feel sorry for refugees who are facing a 90-day delay at a refugee camp in the Middle East. My hair-dresser, who has cut my hair for 25 years, had to stay in Italy as a refugee for 4 months before she was allowed into the United States. Ninety days – boo hoo hoo. To this day, she still has a discernible Russian accent. She is a law-abiding, married mother who works full-time, and who has been doing so continuously for the 25 years I've known her. She owns her own business.

Ninety days? Come on. Get over it.

OBAMA GOT THE NOBEL PEACE PRIZE FOR DOING NOTHING

I know I went over this point, but it bears repeating. Barack Obama was nominated for a Nobel Peace Prize 11 days after he took office. Barack Obama was nominated for a Nobel Peace Prize 11 days after he took office. Barack Obama was nominated for a Nobel Peace Prize 11 days after he took office. Barack Obama was nominated for a Nobel Peace Prize 11 days after he took office. Barack Obama was nominated for a Nobel Peace Prize 11 days after he took office. Way to go, Barry! I guess smoking all those joints paid off.

In the movie, Minority Report, people got arrested for future crimes foreseen by women slaves in a flotation tank called precogs, because they had the power of precognition. In the reality TV show called The Nobel Prizes, Obama was awarded the Peace prize for. . . for what? Why? For future service to humanity? They have precogs in Stockholm? Awarding Obama the Peace Prize was a joke, especially since we're still at war, still doing covert ops in about 70 countries annually, still doing drone strikes, and are still hated by most people in the Muslim world, even after 8 years of peace work by Obama.

There isn't one outcome measure that justifies awarding Obama a Nobel Prize, after 8 years. What were the criteria in 2009? It was 100% political, 100% Democratic lobbying, 100% total bull. Applause, applause, applause from the left side of the aisle. Anyone with any integrity would have declined the Prize. Talk about fake news! It was real news that Obama got the Prize, but it was a fake Prize that he never earned. I didn't see the media asking the tough questions about that one.

Imagine the self-righteous howls that would have gone up if Trump was nominated for a Nobel Peace Prize after 11 days in office! That would have been really ridiculous and embarrassing. But if doing nothing gets you a Nobel Peace Prize these days, then why not Trump? Or me? Or that guy down at the bar? Or the cops that beat Rodney King? Or anybody, I guess, since nothing serious or real happens on reality TV.

BOB DYLAN GOT A NOBEL PRIZE FOR LITERATURE

How many roads must a man walk down, before he gets a Nobel Prize for literature? The answer, my friend, is blowing in the wind, the answer is blowing in the wind. I'm a Dylan fan. Girl From the North Country; I really like it. Hey Mr. Tambourine Man, play a song for me, I'm not sleepy and there ain't no place I'm going to. Actually, I preferred the version by the Byrds, but Dylan still gets credit as the writer. I remember at a Peter, Paul and Mary concert in Winnipeg in the early sixties, they talked about this guy from Hibbing, Minnesota who was setting the world on fire in Greenwich Village. Robert Zimmerman was his birth name. I bet he wasn't real popular at high school, a Jewish nerd like him with a name like that.

So, I like Bob Dylan. I was a little distressed that he and the Beatles didn't remember a single thing about a night they spent together, because they were so stoned. Hey, I could overlook that. But Bob Dylan getting a Nobel Prize for literature? He's on the same level as T.S. Eliot? Come on.

Now two of the Nobel prizes are a joke. This is conclusive evidence of the failure of liberal arts education in the western world. The standards have disintegrated. Now a couple of stoned hippies dancing at Woodstock are "dancers" on the same plane as Nijinsky. Part of the problem is that you can't talk about this problem without getting crucified as an elitist snob. Now even the English professors can't tell the difference between contemporary scribblings and real poetry. Snob, snob, snob. We live in an age of structureless, meaningless free verse, which is all in prose rhythms, and all of no interest to people with real work to do in the world.

The Republicans lose me with their Neanderthal attitudes towards funding the arts, but on the other hand, they have a point. Why should the taxpayer fork out one million dollars for a work of art consisting of a huge canvas painted the same color of orange in its entirety, nothing but the same orange? Who at the Museum of Art makes these decisions? The standards have deteriorated so drastically that there is no point in the taxpayer supporting the so-called artists, or should I say artistes? Let them fund themselves and compete in the market place like everyone else.

On the other hand, why give all the taxpayer goodies to the corporations? Everything given to the artists trickles down into the local economy and generates a multiplier effect, so why not? Maybe that would eat into our military budget, though, which is stretched pretty thin these days.

Bob Dylan getting a Nobel Prize is a symptom, not the problem. How many times can a man turn his head, and pretend that he just doesn't see? The answer, my friend, is blowing in the wind, the answer is blowing in the wind.

THE TAX MAN

Let me tell you how it will be
There's one for you, nineteen for me
'Cause I'm the taxman
Yeah, I'm the taxman

Should five percent appear too small
Be thankful I don't take it all
'Cause I'm the taxman
Yeah, I'm the taxman

Taxman, The Beatles

How many times have I had this conversation? -

"Yeah, it's a great job, because you get paid in cash, so you don't have to pay any taxes on it."

"Oh, cool!"

Here's the IRS formula: the above conversation x millions of times = a lot of tax crime.

That crime against the people has been perpetrated how many times in the United States of America? Millions? Tens of millions? Hundreds of millions? You do the math. These are conversations between working class people, or middle class people, not the top 1% - I'm leaving them out of the conversation for now. The conversation. There's a word that's been mangled by the media in the last five years. A conversation now means a fistfight outside the bar – but it's a verbal fistfight and a virtual bar, probably a radio talk show. It should be illegal to destroy words that way, let alone to take cash under the table and not declare it on your income tax return.

Oh, wait a minute – it is illegal to get paid in cash and not declare it.

In all my years on Planet Earth, I have never met a single person who volunteered to pay more taxes than he or she owed the government. Nor have I met a single person who felt guilty about paying the fewest taxes possible within the law. Nor have I met a single person who felt guilty about taking as many legal deductions as possible.

The honest citizens of America feel fine about tax evasion, as long as it's them doing the evading. Good for me! I damn well worked for it!

Last time I checked, Donald Trump was a citizen of the United States, although he may have been born in Kenya. But when the Donald takes legal deductions on his taxes, oh my oh my oh my, out come the self-righteous knives! It's a Left-Wing Hypocrisy Party and it's an all-nighter! Kool Aid for everyone!

Why on earth would any business person, male or female, left wing or right wing, not take advantage of all available tax deductions? You'd have to be stupid not to do that. I can't believe that a single left-wing self-righteous TV commentator has ever paid a single dollar above the legal minimum taxes. So what does it all boil down to? Jealousy. Vindictiveness. Trump bashing. Hypocrisy. I could think of a few other names for it.

I think I took a year of economics before med school. I think so. Hard to remember, since it was in the Dark Ages. I think I learned something about economics, not left-wing economics, not right-wing economics, just economics. I think when you build a successful business you create a lot of jobs for working and middle-class people that wouldn't exist without you. I think that's right. Not completely sure. And I think you pay a lot of taxes, which helps reduce the national debt, or would if the Federal Government didn't keep racking up more and more debt. I think you create injections into the economy, which create even more jobs through a multiplier effect.

These are very bad things for Donald Trump to have done. Even worse, by reducing his taxes through legal deductions, he was able to retain more dollars and use them for two things: 1) more money for him and his family, and 2) more money for more employees through more jobs he could create resulting in more multiplier effect. This is definitely very bad behavior. It's a disgrace to America that Donald Trump worked hard, was successful, and created financial security for his children, and provided them seed money for their own businesses, just like his father did for him, which he then blew on hookers and coke, like many other spoiled rich kids. Oh, maybe not, maybe he built his seed money into a very successful business. Seems like this kind of misconduct has been going on in the Trump family for generations!

This is what it has come to in America. Hard work, risk taking, and success in business are now crimes against the people. No, no, sorry, I got mixed up – that would be true in the Soviet Union, not in America.

Oh, and just to finish up on taxes – hope this isn't too taxing for you. On March 15, 2017, Rachel Maddow appeared on the Tonight Show with Jimmy Fallon, the day after she scooped the other weanie journalists and released two pages of Trump's 2005 tax return. Man, that's news! The return had been leaked by someone to an intermediary who forwarded it to her. I don't hold a grudge against Rachel, even though she won't go out with me, due to some kind of genetic defect, and much of her conversation with Jimmy Fallon was intelligent and reasonable. She made some valid points, such as: 1) all the other Presidents since Honest Dick Nixon have released their tax returns, and 2) the American people should know whether their President has any conflicts of interests due to prior business dealings and possibly loans from other countries.

That is reasonable, although it takes us to the edge of the abyss known as Trump Russia Bashing. But nevertheless, if Rachel would use the tone, manner and level of argument she used throughout most of that interview, and everyone else in the country would copy her, we would be way ahead of the barbaric mess we're in now. But, surprisingly, Rachel couldn't keep it together. She had to attack Trump for making another Fake News comment in yet another tweet in reaction to her show the previous day, which featured the hot hot hot news of 2 pages of a 2005 tax return. There was Trump again, making another one of his crazy accusations about fake news! He said the tax return was fake news.

OK, but what did Trump actually say in the actual tweet that had actually just been shown to the viewers in large print? He said that the story that an anonymous person had dropped off two pages of his tax return to an investigative journalist wasn't believable. Copies of his tax return don't just materialize from another dimension. He wasn't saying that the tax return itself was fake news. He was saying that the logistics of how it was leaked was fake news. This was crystal clear in his tweet.

Where did Rachel go with that? She pounded her pulpit and said that the authenticity of the tax return had been verified by the White House. She went over how carefully her network, MSNBC, which stands for Men So Not Be Cute, had worked to authenticate the tax return. Why was this necessary? Because, she said, someone could have been playing her and could have sent her a forged document, which would make the whole thing fake news, I guess. MSNBC has to be careful with all this fake news around, she said, but only Donald Trump, the nut case, is worried about fake news. She didn't actually use the term, fake news, but that's what she said.

Rachel followed this with a typical fake news strategy. She attacked Trump for saying that the tax return was fake news, which he never said. The fake news, he said, was the innocent story not implicating anyone on the left, that the tax return had just materialized in an unknown person's hands, and this had nothing to do with any left wing anti-Trump conspirators because Americans never conspire to attack their President, including President Lincoln, as we know. Well, he didn't say that last part about Lincoln – that was just fake news by me.

Rachel then went back to intelligent reasonable mode and said that it's possible that Trump himself could be the source of the leak, since he had access to the return and had the legal right to release it. Anyone releasing it without his consent would be risking prosecution. She also said it was equally possible that someone against Trump had released it. She considered both sides of the issue in a balanced fashion. Way to go, Rach! And way to go, Donald, if it was you who released two pages of an old tax return that showed nothing damaging and proved you are a good guy! Of course if that was the case, then Trump's denial of having released the two pages himself would be fake news.

BIG SATAN AND LITTLE SATAN

This Angel, who is now become a Devil, is my particular friend; we often read the Bible together in its infernal or diabolical sense, which the world shall have if they behave well.

William Blake, The Marriage of Heaven and Hell

You have to admit it - Osama bin Laden was a pretty funny guy! He called America, Satan, and Canada, Little Satan. That's hilarious because it satirizes Canada's self-image of being much more gooder than Evil America. Osama could tell it like it is. Excuse my dyslexia if I mistakenly substitute an 's' for a 'b' in the next sentence. Despite Obama's promise of transparency, his administration set yet another spending record in 2016, breaking the previous record for dollars spent by an administration on the following line item: $36.2 million in legal costs defending its refusal to turn over documents under the Freedom of Information Act, which raised the bar on that category, thanks to help provided by the American Bar Association. Satan is the Father of Lies, as we know. Osama-Obama-Osama-Obama – kind of catchy Colin claims! Osama-Obama-Osama-Obama – mirror, mirror on the wall, who's the biggest Truth Blocker of them all? I dunno. I think maybe Bush, maybe Clinton, maybe Obama, maybe Trump, but maybe there's no difference in that regard, despite their differences in hair styles. Would I lie to you?

Speaking of Little Satan, as a young brainwashee in Canada, I was taught that Canada is everybody's friend, and is respected throughout the world for its diplomacy, peace-keeping and humanitarianism. Apparently not in the caves of Tora Bora. I learned how things work in Canuckville over the years. First, Canada has an inferiority complex and really feels like it's #2 in North America, which it is, however it is helpful to know that you out-rank Mexico in the pecking order. That boosts your self-esteem a little bit.

Canadians were aghast when the US military wanted to test cruise missiles on Canadian soil, back in the day, in the back woods. We ain't like that, you damn Yankees! We don't bomb the shit out of people all over the world. We're polite, we say 'sorry' a lot, and we like to talk things out. Canadians are superior to Americans - we know this to be true due to Canadian reaction formation. America, on the other hand, is so far above Canada that it doesn't even realize there is a competition for first place. Big Satan thanks Little Satan once in a while as long as he delivers lumber, oil, minerals and things of value like that. Never mind about your TV shows, Little Brother. We don't need them.

While Canadians are busy being covertly smug and superior, they simultaneously consume massive amounts of American culture, since their own culture isn't very extravagant or exciting. Canadian reality TV – ho hum. Can't compete with the Trump Card.

I remember when I lived in Winnipeg and used to go to conferences in the United States. Especially if the conference was in the South, I'd always run into the same problem if people asked where I lived. Winnipeg – blank stare. Then I'd say it's just north of North Dakota. Blank stare. Then I tried, it's about 7 hours drive northwest of Minneapolis. Blank stare. Then I gave up. Apparently Minnesota and North Dakota aren't really part of the USA. I think they were just given fake legit status so there could be 50 stars on the flag.

Oh, and then there was the time, back in the sixties, when my friend in Winnipeg reported to an intrepid cub reporter for the Daily Planet, or possibly the Winnipeg Free Press, myself, in the month of July, that some Americans had stopped him and asked where the snow was. They had skis on the top of their car. It's a challenge trying to feel inferior to people like that, but Canadians are up to it, and are saved from oblivion by the fact of their own moral superiority in the mirror of the world, which fools a few people, but definitely not Osama bin, now known affectionately as Dust Bin, since he has been consigned to the dust bin of history. Canada carries on.

Here we have a tale of the devil chasing his tail in a mirror. Canada disavows and disowns its bad self and projects it onto the United States. That way Canada is good. But the procedure is a little trickier than projecting onto Muslims, because Canada and America are such good friends, and Canadians are polite and, after all, one never mentions matters like that in polite society. Underneath, the Canadian dagger is just as sharp as the American one.

OUR REDSKIN BROTHERS BUT WE DON'T CALL THEM REDSKINS

Way, way, way back in the day, the National Indian Brotherhood was the #1 organization in Canada representing Indian rights, run and named by Indians for Indians. It was formed in 1970, and was organizationally preceded by the National Indian Council and Union of B.C. Indian Chiefs. That organization was formed in the Canadian province of British Columbia, not Before Christ, as some American scholars might mistakenly assume. So, in the lifetime of the present scholar, Indians called themselves Indians. This was not a colonialist white conspiracy, unless we say that the Indian rights leaders were still unwitting pawns of the white occupiers. But that in itself would be a colonialist put down of our free-thinking aboriginal brothers, who we love so much because we are inclusive.

When I lived in the Northwest Territories in Canada in the 1970's, I colonialized my native wife into having two kids with me, both of whom have native status in Canada. This was a reverse Trump move: instead of being a male marrying an immigrant, I was a male immigrant to North America marrying a native. I was not a native Canadian, despite the fact that I was a tenth generation Canadian through my French Canadian ancestry on my maternal grandfather's side. Can we assume that Colin Ross is not "against natives"?

I had some non-amusing experiences of being attacked by the left wing, which is pretty far out there in Canada, because of things I wrote about native Canadians. Actually, I was writing about white urban Canadian projections onto the Native Card. Urban white Canadians have provided the world with a beautiful example of reaction formation. Remember, reaction formation is where you take on the opposite set of feelings to what you really feel as a defense against those underlying feelings, which are unacceptable to your self-image, which in this example is being a good white Canadian supporter of Indians rights, except you can't call them Indian rights anymore because that language has become politically unacceptable to Indians, who changed the name of their organization to the Assembly of First Nations in 1982.

Here we have a parallel history to Negroes-Blacks-African Americans.

Since I took out US citizenship, I guess I'm a European American despite the fact that I was born in Canada and am not a native American, let alone a native Canadian, which I guess must mean I'm a native European despite the fact that I was not born in Europe. I think I have it all figured out. In any case, I took some heat from the left back in the 70's because I wasn't endorsing the we love natives here hypocrisy.

What were the facts? The facts were: we never had any Indian wars like you bad Americans because we are good Canadians. What were some other facts?

Indian and Eskimo (whoops, I mean Inuit) cultures have been destroyed in Canada. No native people "live off the land" anymore although some do some hunting. Most young native people in Canada don't speak a native language. The rates of alcoholism, unemployment, violent death and domestic violence are high in native communities, which are actually ghettos except that word is politically incorrect, so we call them native communities, even though no urban white person in his or her right mind would ever, or ever has, set foot in one.

More facts: poor physical and mental health compared to Canadian norms, higher infant mortality, lousier dentition, higher rates of childhood trauma, higher infant mortality, higher suicide rates. But we sure do care about our native brothers, who we isolate behind invisible high wire fences out in the boonies where they won't bother us, on land they own because we gave them a whole bunch of rights and money so we wouldn't feel guilty about hating them underneath on the grounds that they're a bunch of drunken Indians, which we would never say out loud if there is a TV camera anywhere around.

Native Canadians are in the same bad shape as native Americans, after a century-plus of cultural genocide, not to mention some actual genocide, which we also don't talk about because we never had any Indian wars. It wasn't our fault if the Hudson's Bay Company wanted to keep the natives out on the land in their native state so they could trap furs – that was the evil capitalists. Oh no, the Good Catholic Church and the Good Anglican Church herded the native people into small towns so they could make them go to church and stop worshipping pagan gods and forget their language for their own good. Because this plan was approved by Jesus, the Good Canadian Government helped out by building schools and signing treaties with the Indians, who weren't called natives yet.

Originally, the Indians in the Northwest Territories just called themselves Dene, which means "the people" in the Athabaskan language, which is the language group of the Navaho and Apache, who therefore would be immigrants to the United States, except that they arrived in the American Southwest before America was created, sometime between 1200 and 1500 AD, apparently; they got in under the wire before Europeans arrived in North America, at which time the Europeans thought they were in India. By the way, it is still politically correct to call people from India, Indians.

In Evil America, there is an NFL football team called the Washington Redskins and there is a MLB baseball team called the Cleveland Indians. Believe it or not, Mr. Ripley. We sure don't have any sports team names like that in Canada because we love our native brothers and include them in our multi-cultural, tolerant society, although we also ignore them. You see, Canada isn't a melting pot like America, which grinds everybody up into a homogenous soup, no we encourage diversity and have folk festivals every summer to prove it. Canadians believe this propaganda even though there is more diversity in accents among white Americans than there is among white Canadians.

So, the projections of Canadians onto the America Card are another repetition of the themes evident in analysis of the Trump Card. When I was practicing hiding under my school desk in order to survive a direct nuclear strike, in Winnipeg in 1962, who was I relying on to protect my freedom, my democracy, my life, and the sovereignty of my country? That would be Evil America, its military and its Central Intelligence Agency. Being Canadian, I don't have to say thanks for that, because who thanks demons anyway, let alone reads the Bible with them? Only a few Jungian nuts who talk about owning the shadow self. We don't have a shadow in Canada, though we do throw some shade on America once in a while.

INALIENABLE RIGHTS, UFOS, AND OTHER DIMENSIONS

In the United States of America, we are very concerned about rights. We have the Bill of Rights, No Right Turn on Red signs, and 90% of people are right-handed, plus we are always saying, "Right on!", at least we were in recent decades. When we are screwing screws into either wood, metal or plastic, we use primarily a right-handed turn and we have a President who is on the right and therefore is right with America, because Might Makes Right. Also, we like to get right with God because He is our savior and if we don't we might get left behind in Hell, like those left wing people, and having said that there is nothing left to say about left and right.

Therefore let's look at the question of whether Obama wiretapped Trump Tower or not. What do the Democrats have to say about that? It's ridiculous and there's no evidence. But how ridiculous can it be – as a possibility - that Obama wire-tapped Trump when it's a known, publicly acknowledged fact that he tapped Angela Merkel's cell phone? How likely is it that he got caught for the one and only time he conducted illegal surveillance? The accusation that he tapped Trump is perfectly plausible based on prior proven behavior.

And what about Watergate? I realize that is ancient history, but in my lifetime we have publicly documented proof of a President ordering illegal surveillance on Americans in the opposing party. This brings us to the second main pillar in the left-wing proof that Obama did not order surveillance on Trump – there is no evidence. This is an example of the standard logical problem of proving that something never happened, which is always a challenge.

But hold on here, boys and girls. . . who is the left wing quoting as the reliable sources for the conclusion that there is no evidence? Politicians – yep, can trust them. Obama appointees – yep, definitely objective. The FBI and British Intelligence – if I'm not mistaken, their job description is to conduct covert operations and deny that they ever happened. So, really?

Then we have the final flaw in the argument: Obama is so incompetent and has such a leaky security apparatus, that he would have left a clear trail of evidence if he actually did it. Really? That's the left wing's assessment of Obama's ability to set up and run deniable covert operations? It's just not believable. In the end, we don't know if Trump was "tapped" – which could mean any means of covert surveillance. There was no need for a technician to enter Trump Tower and monkey with some wires.

It's a funny diversion, though, to almost imply that Obama personally donned a pair of overalls, entered Trump Tower with a tool box and planted some bugs in the building's electrical or phone system. Way to go, Barry! The whole thing is just one more Trump bashing diversion initiated by Trump. Did it ever occur to you left wing strategists that Trump might be playing you? Oooh! Oooh! Shiny thing! Shiny thing! Let's chase it! Ratings good! Ratings good! Thanks,

Donald, we love hating you.

OK, let's go over it again. Another example of this pattern is the media response to Trump's claim that he had been wire tapped by Obama. Again, Trump makes the statement in such an over-the-top fashion that it sounds ridiculous. The left wing media then gets on him endlessly and reiterates, too many times to count, that there is no evidence of any such wire tapping. Of course, it's impossible that a US President would ever wire tap the opposition, as we learned from Watergate – or no, that's not it, I mean it's impossible that a Democratic President would ever wire tap the opposition, because Democrats belong to the Boy Scouts of America.

But, in any case, where did the wire tap rumors start? In what sector of the fringe conspiracy theory media was this rumor hatched? Answer: in a front-page article in the New York Times on January 20, 2017, entitled, "Wiretapped Data Used in Inquiry of Trump Aides." Say what? According to the article, the reason that Trump aides were accused of consorting with Russians is because their phone conversations with Russians were tapped. The New York Times. Where did this fact get filed by the media over the next six weeks? In the dumpster, forgotten and never mentioned again. Historical amnesia only takes a few days to set in in this country, as far as I remember.

I realize that everyone is busy, that everyone in the media is a busy body, but geez, guys. How about calling for an investigation of The New York Times? Oh, no way, that would be the media policing itself instead of calling for impeachments of Trump, which they do by reporting on other people's calls for impeachment of Trump, because they just report the news. They don't take sides. There are only two options: 1) the media (NY Times) accurately reported the wire tapping of Trump aides based on solid facts, or 2) this was fake news from the mainstream media. Take your pick.

Fake news takes many different forms, one of which is deliberate errors of omission. That's a good tactic because it's hard to impeach someone for not saying something. It's like proving that a crime never happened. No, no crime here. Oh yeah, there was a crime. Oh yeah, prove it! Prove what? I never said there was a crime. Yeah, but you thought it. Thought crimes need to be prosecuted to the full extent of the law, which they are in America, every day, by the anti-Trump press, which keeps up a full-court press on the Donald. Talk about press pressure!

Here's one fact: Donald Trump is the leader of the Free World. . . well, maybe not, but he definitely is the Leader of America. How can you tell? Because when he Trumpets from the White House, everyone dances to his tune, either in the Yes Camp or the No Camp. Trump takes it over the top and the media ratchets the pressure up another notch! It's all good for the ratings.

The media loves the Trump Card; that's why they follow suit.

Oh, one more fact. After weeks of ridiculing Trump, the media reported that in fact the FBI did do wire taps at Trump Tower, from 2011 to 2013, with a judicial warrant. They tapped a bunch of Russians three floors below Donald Trump's penthouse, resulting in indictments of 30 people. On April, 2013, subsequent to an FBI raid on Trump Towers. Vadim Trincher, a Russian businessman who had been living on the 63rd floor of Trump Tower, was sentenced to five years in jail as a result of this operation. All of this was reported by ABC and other major news outlets in 2013.

For weeks while Trump was being bashed for his unproven allegations that Obama had tapped him, this 2013 story was not mentioned. Then all of a sudden it popped up in the news one day in March, 2017. Why? How? Who made that decision? Was this just random, or was it orchestrated? I have no idea. But I know one thing: it is a fact that the Government of the United States has conducted wire-tapping operations in Trump Tower, three floors below the penthouse in which Donald Trump lives. Maybe, just maybe, Trump could have a point. Maybe his allegation wasn't quite so far-fetched as the media made out.

Hold on, hold on: breaking news! On March 22, 2017, Republican Rep. Devin Nunes, Chairman of the House Intelligence Committee said in a statement to reporters that communications by Trump's staff had been wire-tapped by the FBI from November, 2016 to January 2017, as part of their ongoing investigation into Russian organized crime. So Trump isn't paranoid at all. He's just been stating the facts. The only remaining question is whether Obama was witting or unwitting – obviously, if he was in the loop, all his soldiers will say, "No, he wasn't."

Why did this information come out in March, you might ask, and I do ask? Just a guess here: it looks to me like it's part of the ongoing campaign to attack Trump with the Buddy of Putin strategy. Every hint of a connection to Russia, even if it's only an investigation of a possible connection, paints the ugly picture of the Russian Trumpster Who Should Be In the Dumpster = be impeached.

But back to aliens. We need to re-examine our immigration policy to include extra-planetary arrivees, if we are going to be truly inclusive. Aliens should have certain inalienable rights, to due process, refugee benefits, free ice cream, and other essentials for survival in America. Or, on the other hand, maybe we should initiate a 90-day pause – which the left could call a ban – because we sure as heck have control over our borders. Notice Trump didn't try to implement a 90-day pause on immigration from Mexico? Why? Because we don't have control over the US-Mexico border, so there would be no point. Without a wall, the rapists, murderers and drug dealers just keep pouring in. Sadly, the left has to admit, the country whose immigrants have perpetrated by far the most crime and death in the US is Mexico. That's just a fact. But the left won't admit it, instead they spin it into more Trump bashing as a diversion from a conversation about that uncomfortable fact.

If you mention that uncomfortable fact, you get attacked by the left as a xenophobe racist, because the left doesn't actually want to solve problems and deal with the facts, which makes them indistinguishable from the right in the Washington gridlock. I mean, look at these politicians – they're mostly white, mostly male, all at least upper middle class, mostly urban, mostly college educated, mostly Christian – they have more in common with each other than they have differences, not to mention their sweet pensions and health care.

Aliens are so excluded from "the conversation" that we don't even mention them in conversations on TV about immigration, but that omission should itself be part of the conversation. Whether aliens exist or not is not even part of the conversation. I remember when I had a Green Card that said Resident Alien on it – this was during the Men in Black era. I told a kid I was talking to that I was an alien and I had the government identification to prove it. He was skeptical, but he had heard of INS Division 6 and I explained that they had processed my arrival on Earth. He was still skeptical, and then I showed him my Green Card – his eyes got very very wide and he believed me 100%, a misperception of which I did not disabuse him prior to my departure from his vicinity.

This is why I can speak with authority on the topic of whether aliens should have inalienable rights, which they should. I can prove that because I was an alien myself before I got citizenship, so try walking a mile in my space boots.

I also remember watching an episode of Outer Limits on our black and white TV, which is where I learned the logic of black and white thinking. A man was boarding with a normal American family and explained to them that he was from another planet and was being pursued by criminals from his home planet, which is why he was trying to remain discretely anonymous on earth.

Then, the family cat walked by and the alien looked at it and said, "Where?"

The cat looked at the wall and suddenly a dimensional portal opened and a bounty hunter from that planet emerged into the living room. It turned out that the original arrivee was the criminal. From this episode I learned that cats are in fact capable of several different paranormal feats, including precognition and mental telepathy. I also learned that you can't keep aliens out by building a wall.

TRUMP'S KILLING GRANNY, TRUMP'S KILLING GRANNY

You'd think the populace would have been busy with March Madness in March, 2017, and they were, but there was still enough spare time to be in an uproar about Trump's planning to cut Meals on Wheels, which was itself a form of March madness. There were heart-wrenching interviews with shut-in seniors who would be facing death by starvation when the inhumane Trump budget cuts took effect. This was fake news.

What were the facts? The facts were: Meals on Wheels receives 3% of its funding from the Federal government. The maximum hit to Meals on Wheels from Trump budget cuts could be 3%. But the news coverage – from the left, surprise, surprise – made it sound like the entire Meals on Wheels operation was going to be shut down. Trump's Killing Granny! Trump's Killing Granny!

Here is a fact: it was unlikely, in March, 2017, that even this 3% of the Meals on Wheels budget would be cut by the Evil Donald, because the proposed cut was to the Community Development Block Grant program administered through the Department of Housing and Urban Development. Most of the federal funding for Meals on Wheels comes from Health and Human Services, according Meals On Wheels Vice President of Communications, Jenny Bertolette.

Here's a fact: Trump cutting Meals on Wheels was 100% left-wing propaganda, aka, fake news. When Trump complains about fake news, however, he gets nailed for being a nut, which could be true news, but that doesn't let the fake news partisan journalists off the hook.

This is what I mean about the failure of liberal arts education in the western world. The ability to think critically, to weigh evidence, to evaluate the facts, and to account for bias in oneself and others is moribund, which means not doing real good. This is fertile ground for controlling the populace with propaganda, which is in turn fertile ground for establishing a totalitarian police state, be it left wing or right wing. As mentioned previously, the scales of justice seem currently to be tipping towards a tipping point to the left, after which there will be nothing left of America because everything will have gone so far left there's no room to be further left at that point, if you take my point.

Et tu, Brute.

GRANNY MADE IT, BUT TRUMP'S KILLING HER AGAIN

Boy, that was a close call for Granny! But, but, oh no – Trump's killing her again! This time the axe he's using is his health care plan. I've heard it over and over, during March madness, that the Trump plan will result in 24 million people losing health insurance. The commentators always make it sound like this will happen immediately and people will be dying in 2017 as a result.

What's that concept again? Oh yeah, fake news. In this example, the facts are sort of correct but are so spun in the anti-Trump direction that they create a fake news impression. This tactic from the left is the same fear-mongering for which they berated Trump in particular, and the Republicans in general, during the 2016 campaign. Exactly the same tactic.

What's that other concept? Oh yeah, the facts. When you try to read the Congressional Budget Office (CBO) analyses, as reported in the media, it immediately becomes apparent that there are a lot of assumptions and projections involved. One of these projections is that the number of uninsured will go up compared to Obamacare. OK, but how much over what time period? And what assumptions are involved? How about if we analyze and discuss instead of emotionally reacting based on perceptions, that is, projections onto the Trump Card?

According to the CBO analyses, under the Trump health care plan, which wasn't even finalized as of the CBO projections, the number of uninsured would rise to 52 million by 2026. Right. But where does the 24 million number come from, then? Why are the left wing zingers giving Trump a break and only saying 24 million? Just to clear up any residual confusion, I'm talking About Evil Trumpcare versus Good Obamacare. Got it? Obama good, Trump bad.

Well, surprise, surprise, over-reacting public, according to the CBO, under Obamacare the number of uninsured will rise to 28 million by 2026 – if no change is made to the law. No change. This is the projection if we keep Obamacare. 52-28 = 24. This is where the 24 million number comes from. So Obamacare is evil too, but less so than Trumpcare. It's not two separate categories: black versus white, good versus evil, Obama versus Trump. Both plans suck horribly, both leave at least 28 million Americans uninsured by 2026, and the Trump plan is just a somewhat worse version of Obamacare in that regard.

Another fact: most of the increase in the uninsured between 2018 and 2026, according to the CBO projections, would result from cuts by State Medicaid programs. It's not even a direct cut by the Feds under either Trumpcare or Obamacare. Of course, the argument there is that the State cuts will be forced on the States by cuts in federal transfer payments. But I get it, Trump evil, Obama good.

But anyway, it's all irrelevant now, thanks to the Democratic God! Granny escaped the axe one more time! Trump found out a key difference between the business world and Washington politics during his health care negotiations: business people actually want to make deals and get things done; Washington politicians don't. You can't negotiate with someone who does not want to make a deal, and won't budge or move one millimeter to get a deal done.

MORE JOBS IN AMERICA IS BAD

On March 15, 2017 – smack in the middle of March madness – President Trump gave a speech to autoworkers in Michigan. He got a positive response because he reiterated his plan to bring manufacturing jobs back to America, to level the international trading field through tariffs, taxes and other mechanisms so that American car companies could compete with foreign companies in the US market and abroad, and to stimulate growth in the US car industry.

I don't see why these goals are bad for America, or why Democrats have to condemn them. They are good goals for American workers and for all the industries that supply parts, services, repairs, sales, marketing and a host of other functions for American-built cars. This would have a substantial multiplier effect, possibly even a big, beautiful multiplier effect.

Maybe, instead of knee-jerk opposition to Trump and the Republicans at every turn, we could consider analysis, rational argument, tradeoffs, cost-benefits and such. Look in the mirror, Democrats – you are behaving exactly like the Republicans did during the Obama administration. During those 8 years, the Republicans became The Party of No. They said 'no' to everything Obama wanted to do, automatically. They got so bogged down in the psychology of 'no' that they even said 'no' to their own Presidential candidate once he became their nominee. The grumpy Republicans said that Trump wasn't their nominee before the election just like the grumpy Democrats said he wasn't their President after the election.

Speaking of cost-benefit, what is the counter-balancing consideration? The environment. Trump, in March, 2017, was proposing a review of EPA emissions and gas mileage standards set up by the Obama administration. Trump said that these were imposing excessive costs on the car industry and driving car-manufacturing jobs out of the country. He also said that the standards were set when projections about gas prices and penetration of the car market by electric cars were different from current projections – the projections have been updated, but the policy hasn't. That sounds reasonable – what's wrong with reconsidering based on evolving economic projections?

Trump is Killing Grandmother Willow! That's the call that goes up from the left wing and the environmentalists. Trump bad, Obama good! I value the environment as much as anyone. I'm pro-environment all the way. But don't these things have to be balanced? We could protect the environment best by going back to the Stone Age, but I assume the Democratic Party isn't recommending that course of action. So where is the balance in the middle? Jobs versus environmental protection?

The world's coral reefs are dying. I like scuba diving. I don't want the reefs to die. But how can we strike a balance? Is Trump too far out of balance one way? Are the extreme environmentalists too far out of balance in the opposite direction? How do we decide? The American way is by drive-by shootings, it seems, at a verbal and political level. And there we have the problem, yet again – partisan emotional reactions driven by limbic system over-ride of the cerebral cortex. Bring it on! Ramp it up! Watch the TV ratings soar!

TV ratings. Huh. That would be evil, giant corporations, right? How are ratings generated? You gotta get people to turn on, tune in and drop out of any serious activities – I'm talking about the American Politics Reality TV Show, starring Donald Trump. The more outrageous his manner, tweets and statements, the bigger the self-righteous reaction on the left, which eggs the Donald on, which results in yet more outrageous tweets, which results in more over-reactions on the left, all of which has to be commented on by the left wing and the right wing commentators, and on and on it goes.

Welcome, left wing anti-Trumpers! You're part of the Show! Your behavior is cranking up the ratings which cranks up the profits for the big media corporations. They don't mind. Bash away! Welcome to Hollywood! Corporate America thanks you!

DEPORTING CARTEL CRIMINALS IS BAD

According to the Democrats, it's a good thing to import as many rapists, murderers and drug dealers into America as possible. This is part of NAFTA, the North American Free Trade Agreement, it seems. Or did I misunderstand? Is it actually good for women in Texas, Arizona and California to get raped by Mexican drug gangs? Is it really good for more and more American kids to get hooked on drugs?

Maybe not. If not, what's the left wing plan for dealing with this very serious problem? According to the left, Trump immigration policy is just like Trump budget cuts - bad, bad, bad. But what about the deficit? It grew around $10 trillion under Obama. How is that not bad for America? What is the left wing plan for cutting the deficit? There doesn't seem to be one, as far as I can see. The plan is to just keep on spending. Now the Democrats have become The Party of No. They say 'no' to any and all budget cuts by Trump, automatically, without proposing an alternative solution.

This doesn't mean that the Trump budget plan is good. For example, his cuts seem to be offset by increases in military spending. But automatically saying 'no' to Trump just keeps the whole thing going around in circles. It doesn't solve anything.

In the second edition of my textbook, Dissociative Identity Disorder. Diagnosis, Clinical Features and Treatment of Multiple Personality (1997), I wrote about errors of logic and scholarship committed by extreme skeptics, of whom there were a few, and of which there were many. The entire debacle of a pseudo-debate about multiple personality disorder was symptomatic of a larger problem, the pervasive failures of scholarship, and the low levels of intellectual function in psychiatry, which are in turn symptomatic of a pervasive problem in western civilization. One of the rhetorical strategies of extreme skeptics, I called the extreme case escalation tactic. In the extreme case escalation tactic, a statistical outlier within a category is used to invalidate the entire category.

In the extreme case escalation tactic – which is widely used in American politics and American political commentary – a person runs the "conversation" up the flag pole to the highest height possible, describes the most ultra-extreme example from the other side, and then uses the extreme case to invalidate everything the opposing side has said or done. So, if one Republican makes some ultra-crazy statement about homosexuality or the Bible or the environment or whatever, the opposing Democrat pounds on his desk with his shoe, ramps up the righteous indignation, and dismisses the entire Republican party based on the one extreme example. The Democrat can't help it – the rules of public discourse were set up for him by Nikita Kruschev. He's just following the rules.

Trump plays right into this, of course, either by strategy or by simple buffoonery, which keeps the Democrats spinning. Thus, and thusly, once Trump says that Mexican rapists and murderers are coming in over the border without documentation, it's game over. From that moment on, everything he says is xenophobic monster behavior, racism, intolerance, on and on and on. It doesn't matter how many times Trump points out that he employs Mexicans, that he loves Mexicans, that he respects the Mexican people, he is frozen in carbonite forever.

But what are the facts? Does anyone – pro-Trump or anti-Trump – know? How many rapes and murders are committed by illegal Mexicans in the United States per year? How many drugs are sold? And how do the rates of these crimes among illegal Mexican immigrants compare to the rates among legal Mexican immigrants? And, in turn, how do those rates compare to the rates among American-born people of different races? Would we want to have any such facts available when formulating policy? Or should policies be based solely on uninformed emotional reactions and the extreme case escalation tactic?

What if American-born African-Americans commit more rapes, murders and robberies per capita than illegal Mexican immigrants? Would that mean we should deport them to Africa? Obviously not. What if illegal Mexicans commit more such crimes than African-Americans? Should we deport the Mexicans? Maybe. We could at least consider that option, but no, all discussion gets silenced by left wing hollering. But we end up doing something, even if we do nothing. If we do nothing, then our policy is that illegal Mexican criminals can stay.

The whole Show is a diversion from talking in a reasonable manner about very complicated problems that have no easy solution. Dismissing the mothers of children who have been raped, murdered or addicted to drugs by illegal Mexicans is itself an inhumane form of discrimination. Maybe people who want to deport undocumented Mexican criminals are trying to protect American women and children of all races, not to mention non-criminal illegal aliens. Why is this a bad thing?

All illegal Mexicans have to go is as absurd as all illegal Mexicans get to stay. Could we try to find some common ground in the middle, instead of patrolling the hood heavily armed? Why don't we start with what we agree on, and build from there, instead of defaulting to the extreme case escalation tactic at every turn? Maybe we should consider the possibility that we don't have to hate and demonize someone just because he or she disagrees with us. The tolerant left is incredibly intolerant of the right these days. Vice versa in the mirror the right is looking into.

REDUCED DRUG PRICES FOR SENIORS ARE REALLY BAD

Big Pharma had a sweet deal under the Obama administration, which was basically the same deal as under the Bush and Clinton administrations, which takes us back to ancient history. Medicare pays a fortune in excess drug costs every year. Why? Because the Big Pharma lobbyists bought the politicians, just like they bought psychiatry. This is straight up diversion of taxpayer money to big business. The chain of custody of the dollars goes: taxpayer-IRS-general federal revenue-drug companies.

While this charming transaction was being repeated to the tune of billions of dollars per year, the insurance companies were running the same scam. They paid big dollars for drugs due to the economy being rigged by the federal government, but they didn't mind, because they passed the costs onto the consumers = the taxpayers. How did the chain of custody of those dollars work? Taxpayer-insurance company-drug company. The insurance company lobbyists are also big dogs on Capitol Hill, which should be renamed Capital Hill, since all our capital is going to the capitol for redistribution to big business.

I didn't hear Obama or Hillary or Bernie talking about reducing Medicare drug costs. That might make people on Wall Street angry, which definitely could impact your speaking fees. This is one potential benefit of having a financially independent, non-career politician in the White House, a President who hasn't been bought. But no, Trump all bad. Wouldn't that be ironic if Trump ended up doing more to reduce unnecessary drug profits in America than his two predecessors. The Democrats could figure out some way to demonize such an accomplishment, however, so nothing to worry about there.

I guess you could argue that Big Pharma needs the Big Prices because it costs so much to develop drugs these days. That's what Big Pharma already says. For some reason, they forget to mention that 65% of their budget goes to marketing. And marketing, as we know, is big business, so the taxpayer has to fund it too.

TRUMP AND HIS BUDDY JUSTIN TRUDEAU

Who knows? Trump and Trudeau might become BFFs one day. I doubt it, though, because Trump isn't very good at yoga. But Canada and America are indeed BFFs, even though Canada fools around with the Queen on the side. Actually, however, as we know, Canada is a Communist state, so Trump being buddies with Trudeau is just as bad as his being buddies with Putin.

Actually, in my opinion, the relationship between Big Satan and Little Satan is a model for the world. The relationship may not be completely healthy, but then no one comes from a completely normal family. They don't exist. Sure, sure, the relationship is a little neurotic and Little Satan feels a little insecure about it and compensates with projection and reaction formation, but really it's a normal level of neurosis.

The relationship between Canada and the United States is a lot healthier than the relationship between the United States and itself.

You don't see Canadian politicians trash-talking America in TV interviews every day of the week, and vice versa for American politicians. Likewise, you don't hear regular Canadian citizens trash-talking Americans in public every day of the week, and vice versa for Americans. But Democrats trash-talking Republicans, that you do hear every day of the week, from politicians to TV commentators to regular citizens.

I hold an American passport and a Canadian passport. I don't have a Canadian self who hates my American self, or vice versa, even on Boxing Day.

Hey, American Gringos, why don't you try treating each other the way Canada and America treat each other? Just a thought. I'm not saying American hockey teams should have a right to win the Stanley Cup. . . or no, I guess I am. Now that I think about it, I guess it's OK that we have European and Russian import players in the NHL. They make our game better, more competitive, and more fun to watch.

THE BAIT AND DON'T SWITCH INTERVIEW TECHNIQUE

"When y'er fishin' fer catfish, ya gotta use the right bait, that's fer darn sure."

"Basil, Basil, there seems to be a foreigner in the Club. Most irregular."

"Quite, Cecil, quite. I'll have my man take care of it."

Over and over and over, I've seen the same interview technique, whatever the network and whatever the program: baiting, baiting, baiting. I'm waiting, waiting, waiting for some something to change, but I'm not holding, holding, holding my breath.

It doesn't matter what the topic is, the conversation will be going on and all of a sudden the interviewer throws in a hook with a big, beautiful worm on it, hoping the fish will take the bait. The bait may be out of context or may be connected to the topic of conversation. Let's say the interviewer is talking with a politician about a speech given by a female politician from the opposing party. The speech might have dealt with a fiscal policy.

The interviewer will say, "Isn't it true you tried to put your hand up her dress?"

Or, if the politician whose speech is being discussed is male, the question might be, "Didn't your wife have an affair with him last week?"

The content of the conversation is irrelevant. It's just an opportunity to provoke an emotional over-reaction, which is a set-up for interviewing the politician whose speech was just commented on in the next segment, so he or she can have an emotional over-reaction to the previous over-reaction.

The problem isn't whether the interviewer or interviewee is a Democrat or a Republican. It doesn't matter. It's all about what gets the ratings. There has to be a tabloid scandal. Someone has to be outraged, someone has to get trolled, and the little kid in the second aisle sits back and watches what he or she has provoked, in the third grade classroom, with a self-righteous smirk. Even Smurfs don't behave that badly.

YELLOW JOURNALISM AND PALE YELLOW JOURNALISM

Did you read that book, The Yellow River by I.P. Nightly?

We thought that was a pretty funny joke, in Grade Four in Winnipeg, Manitoba, one of the cultural hot spots in the western world at that time.

What exactly is yellow journalism? It's a synonym for American journalism. It means tabloid pabulum. It means contemporary journalism ain't worth. . . well, you get the idea. But, of course, there are good journalists. I'm talking about the dominant tone on TV and the internet, which is sensationalism to the max.

When a dog bites a man, that's not news, but when a man bites a dog, now that's news (the preceding was a wise saying from Canada in the 1950's). Which reminds me, I remember when we didn't have a television and I had to go to my friend's home down the street to watch TV on Saturday mornings. But then we did get a TV, black and white, of course, with 2 or 3 channels. I remember our party line phone. And I remember adjusting our rabbit ears, which could be very frustrating. Then reel-to-reel tape recorders – I used mine a ton! Then cassette tapes. 33's, 45's and 78's. Color TV somewhere in there, Beta tapes, then VHS tapes, then CDs and DVDs, cell phones, then a crazy little thing called the internet, then live streaming. I don't remember holographic movies because they haven't happened yet, but they're coming.

In the course of all this incredible development, what has happened to the standards of journalism in America? Downhill by the decade. It's very interesting to read an American newspaper from the early twentieth century. You pick it up and start in on an article, and soon find out that it is an intelligently written essay, undergraduate college level stuff. Pick up a newspaper today and you're a dinosaur, but if you do, what will you find? The reading level has gone down 5-6-7 grades.

How often do you look online and find a sensational headline? Every day. I remember one announcing that scientists had found the gene for prostate cancer. I knew that was scientifically impossible, so I read on just for the fun of finding the flaws in the headline. Ten-plus paragraphs in, I found it: the gene in question occurs in 4% of cases. Ho hum. Since that's such a boring finding, it has to be dressed up in the headline as exciting, breaking news.

It's the same thing in political reporting. So and so said such and such, then you read down and find out that's not really what he said, or he did, but it meant something different in context, or the person was stating a hypothetical, or something of the sort. This is standard operating procedure in journalism now.

Here is a guaranteed way to tell if you're being exposed to yellow journalism: if the person claims to be asking the hard questions, you can be sure he or she is not. The hard questions! Are you kidding me? This is why I am writing this writing from a meta-position, in this case, down dog. I'm trying to stay above the fray, not taking one side or the other in the partisan gang war, which is being fought in the corridors of Capitol Hill, rather than out on the streets where honest people fight.

Being involved in "the political process" in America doesn't necessarily mean you are actually getting anything done. It may, but on the other hand, maybe you are just perpetuating the endless partisan squabbling that has gotten very, very far out of control in America. We change America every 4 to 8 years, but nothing ever changes. Nobody destroys America and nobody saves America, in Washington. Repeat advice to terrorists: save yourself some energy and let America continue to destroy itself from within. The whole thing will be on the News.

STRATEGY NUMBER ONE: ACCUSE YOUR ENEMY OF WHAT YOU YOURSELF DO

I got an overdose of this strategy during the False Memory wars in the 1990's, so I'm pretty good at spotting it. In partisan politics, the strategy plays a very big, beautiful role. It builds a big, beautiful wall between the Democrats and the Republicans. It's funny that Trump is proposing to build a wall on the edge of America, when actually he needs to break down a wall in Washington, which may be humanly impossible, but that only matters if Trump is in fact human. If he's some kind of android, maybe he can get it done.

For example, the left wing accuses Trump of being xenophobic, but they are xenophobic towards Trump. The left wing accuses the right wing of being intolerant, but they have no tolerance for the right. Both sides accuse the other of destroying America, but what is destroying America is the intolerance, emotional over-reactivity, dumbing down, hypocrisy, and self-serving self-righteousness that dominates both sides of the aisle and all interactions between the two sides.

It's like the Hatfields and the McCoys are sitting on opposite sides of the church while a male Hatfield is marrying a female McCoy, or vice versa. In the Middle East, this takes the form of the Sunnis versus the Shiites, so America and the Middle East are pretty much the same with regards to their internal warfare. Nice going, Amerika!

Both sides have God on their side, both say God Bless America, but both are praying to God to bless only their half of America, because the other half deserves to go to Hell. The right wing gets a little bit more literal and Biblical about their feelings, but it's the same feelings on both sides.

Another example: the far right wing wants to get rid of birth control and abortion. OK, sure, but then who is going to support the children? A bunch of lazy single mothers living off of welfare, I suppose, while hard-working men go out and earn an honest dollar and impregnate whomever they want whenever they want but take no responsibility for their progeny or the dispersal of their DNA into the gene pool. This attitude makes sense if you're masturbating at a sex show somewhere in one of those little rooms with a screen that stays up so you can watch a naked woman through the glass as long as you keep putting money in which is hard to do when your hands are working so hard keeping you hard, but it doesn't make sense when you have fathered a child.

In any case, the extreme right wing doesn't care about the mother or the child.

Everything is completely different on the far left. Oh, oh, I'm starting to get déjà vu, or is it deja ecrit? A woman should have total control over her own body and her own health care decisions, and she should be able to get an abortion anytime she likes and the father should have no right to block the abortion. However, if she decides to keep the baby, he sure as hell should pay child support. The attitudes are actually mirror opposites of each other. The child is disposable either way.

On the right, the man gets to deposit his sperm but doesn't have to deposit any money. On the left, the man gets to deposit his sperm and doesn't have to deposit any money as long as momma gets an abortion, which is fine with him.

THAT HORRIBLE DSM-5: HYPOCRISY ON THE LEFT

The same conflicts, themes, transactional patterns etc., etc., etc., dominate the mental health field much like they dominate politics. In psychiatry, it's the biological psychiatrists versus the psychoanalysts. It's an internal religious war with the biological shrinks claiming to be scientists and the psychoanalysts claiming to take a human approach. The thought processes in both camps are pretty much the same – both sides believe their ideology in the absence of scientific proof, and both sides do so dogmatically and fervently, or possibly fermentively, depending on how you actually spell that word. The biological psychiatrists claim that they have evidence, but in fact their ideology is disproven by the evidence in psychiatry journals. They are not evidence-based, they are anti-evidence-based.

On the psychotherapy side of the aisle, the Good Humans tend to be pretty left wing. I remember being at a conference once where a clearly far left wing woman, likely lesbian, definitely feminist, not very attractive, in rather ugly clothing, was ranting on about psychiatrists. Surprise, surprise, she said that they're a bunch of male chauvinists (which is true) and all they care about is controlling everyone and earning more than they should, which is not necessarily more than that woman should earn, I assume, since she is a Good Human.

After a few paragraphs, the rant turned to DSM-IV (DSM-5 hadn't come out yet). Again, surprise, surprise, she said that DSM-IV was a male chauvinist abomination that medicalizes everything so psychiatrists can control everything and control her and control the money and be exactly like her dad, I imagine. It is in fact true that DSM-IV and DSM-5 medicalize everything. So what's my problem with this woman? Not to mention the entire audience, which was eating it up, due to their binge eating disorders.

I raised my hand and tried to make a point, but before I had finished, the temperature in the room had already dropped 20° F. It seemed that my words had provoked a chill. What did I say? I tried to point out that there was a problem: everyone in the room was a mental health professional working in the mental health field to treat mental disorders. If their clients didn't have mental disorders as defined by DSM-IV and if they didn't record a DSM-IV diagnosis on their billing sheets, none of them would get paid. Everyone in the room lived off of insurance companies, the government, NGOs, or whoever, but in all instances a DSM-IV diagnosis was required in order for the Good Human therapists to get paid. They were all living off the DSM-IV while being holier-than-thou about it.

I made my point calmly in professional language, saying that this was something that needs to be talked about (an easy sell when the potential buyer is a therapist, you would think). Weren't no Good Humans buying my product on that day, I can tell you.

There is a big problem in the psychotherapy sector of the mental health field. Except for CBT and its variants (CBT = cognitive-behavioral therapy), plus EMDR Therapy and a few other methods or models, a lot of psychotherapy isn't very evidence-based. Yet, these non-evidence-based therapists feel no obligation to do treatment outcome studies, even though they bill third parties for most of their services, the only exception being self-pay clients, who pay out of their pockets, but who are a minority of clients.

Why should a third party pay for a mental health service of no proven benefit? Basically, because the Good Humans have God on their side, and what they do is holy and good. Little do the Good Humans realize that they are sowing the seeds of their own destruction, because the tap is going to get shut off sometime.

I'll bet you that most psychotherapy treatment outcome studies are conducted by people to the right of middle on the political spectrum. I'll bet you that CBT therapists tend to be more right wing than touchy feely do-gooder therapists. And I'll bet you that the reluctance to do treatment outcome studies goes up as the effectiveness of the therapy goes down. In other words, the two are inversely correlated. I rest my case. Oh and pill-pushing psychiatrists tend to be more right wing too. OK, now I rest. I pray the Lord my soul to keep.

COLIN ATTACK! COLIN ATTACK! (ROSS NOT POWELL)

So, to samuraize, what are the basic points, arguments, theses, themes, or sword strokes of this book, given that I'm adhering to the sage principle of bringing a sword for the cause of peace? The pen is mightier than the sword, which is why I wield a metaphorical sword, unlike the Kyozu swordsman played by Seiji Miyaguchi in The Seven Samurai, which is one of my favorite films. I greatly admire his warrior spirit, his discipline, his physical skill, and his utterly non-macho energy. He and Dersu Uzala are two of my favorite characters in all of cinema, both directed by Akira Kurosawa.

If this book was a Colin Powell attack, then America would be getting a High Colonic Enema. But I'm not a gastroenterologist, I'm a psychiatrist, so this is just a mental cleanse. Call it a Colinalaysis. Patients at one of the hospitals I work at call a therapy session with me a ColinRosscopy – funny folks!

But what are my main points in this here diatribe (a diatribe is a small group of aboriginals depicted in a diorama at a museum, in case you don't know that word)? My points are:

1. The ramped up bipartisan hatred in America needs to settle down, boys and girls.
2. There is a lot of fake news around.
3. Trump is playing you, left-wingers. His ridiculous, ramped up over-reactions generate counter-ramped counter-reactions by you, which is how he got elected.
4. The extremes at both ends of the political spectrum are equally dangerous and ridiculous.
5. The standards of discourse in America are in the dumpster, along with intellectual standards.
6. It's fun writing political satire.

That pretty well sums it up.

WHY DID WE INVADE IRAQ? FAKE INTEL

Oh, never mind. I already covered that.

WE DID WE INVADE GRENADA?

Oh, never mind. I already covered that.

FAKE NEWS: THE WASHINGTON MUTUAL COLLAPSE

As reported in the mainstream media, Washington Mutual had assets of $307 billion on June 30, 2008. It had liabilities of about $271 billion for a net value of $36 billion. In September, 2008, customers began a run on the bank, withdrawing $16.7 billion over nine days. On the evening of Thursday, September 25, 2008 the Federal Government, through the Office of Thrift Supervision, seized the bank. This was done to prevent the collapse of the bank. It was also a good move for the citizens of that banana republic, the United States of America. This happens in banana republics – the government seizes private businesses without any legal process.

Given all the financial stress of 2008, the Thursday seizure of WaMu was good news for the American taxpayer, which all of a sudden had acquired an asset of $36 billion for free. There was a hitch, however. The Federal Deposit Insurance Corporation (FDIC), which had assets of $45.2 billion, was potentially on the hook for $30 billion in WaMu debt if the bank collapsed. This would be bad for Big Brother. So what did the federal government (government of the people, for the people and by the people) do?

On Sunday, September 28, the government sold Washington Mutual to JP Morgan for $1.9 billion. As part of this deal, the FDIC liability of $30 billion was erased and Big Bro was off the hook. All of this was real news and was reported accurately by the mainstream media. All good.

But wait a sec! We The People held an asset of $36 billion and sold it for $1.9 billion after three days? A sweet deal for JP Morgan! The fake news was the fact that the mainstream media never said boo. The analysts analyzed, the commentators commented, the hosts hosted, the reporters reported, but nobody said boo. How did this deal make sense? It made sense for the FDIC and it sure made sense for JP Morgan. Even if We The People assumed the $30 billion FDIC liability, we would still have had a net asset of $6 billion.

Clearly, this was a back room deal, and insider trading. No comment on that by the media. We'll fake it that we're reporting and analyzing and commenting, but no one will point to the elephant in the room. I'm not an economist, and maybe there is an explanation of why we sold our asset at such a low price, an explanation that makes sense for us. I doubt it, but maybe. When it comes down to it, big media isn't likely to blow the whistle on big banking. I call it

Fake News Variation Number 17 and it's one of my favorite compositions.

FAKE NEWS: RAYMOND LEE HARVEY AND OSVALDO ORTIZ

Here's another example of real fake news in the mainstream media. On May 5, 1979, Jimmy Carter was scheduled to give a speech to a Latino audience at the Los Angeles Civic Center Mall. There was a disturbance in the crowd and two men were arrested. They told investigators that they had been recruited by three Mexicans the day before and had been assigned the job of creating a diversion in the crowd using blank rounds in pistols. Carter would then be assassinated by one of the men who had recruited them. The pistols were confiscated by the police and the two men were arrested and interrogated.

According to the two men, they had never met before they were recruited by "Julio" – on the evening of May 4, they had practiced shooting blanks from the roof of the hotel where Julio was staying, the Alan Hotel. When authorities went to the room rented under the name, Umberto Comacho, they found a shotgun case and several rounds of ammunition. In some reports, Julio was one of the men, a Mexican illegal immigrant, arrested in the crowd, in others he was the shooter who rented the room, and in some accounts he left behind a shotgun case, in others a rifle case. But the story was reported in the mainstream media.

The men's names, which were reported in the mainstream media, were Raymond Lee Harvey and Osvaldo Ortiz. The mainstream commentators shrugged this off as an odd coincidence. It was indeed odd, given that Raymond Shaw is the mind-controlled assassin shooter in The Manchurian Candidate.

So here is the real news we are supposed to believe, and no one in the mainstream questions it: on November 22, 1963, JFK was assassinated by Lee Harvey Oswald. On May 5, 1979, Raymond Lee Harvey and Osvaldo Ortiz were part of an attempt to assassinate Jimmy Carter. The names were pure coincidence. Raymond Lee Harvey was an American drifter from Ohio and Osvaldo Ortiz was an illegal Mexican immigrant, and they had never met till May 4, and they both just happened to be in LA at that time. They were arrested but then released for lack of evidence and disappeared, with no follow-up by the mainstream media.

If you're willing to believe that story, I give up. You'll buy anything. It's a real news fake news story – it's fake because there was no real investigative reporting of what actually happened there. I doubt that Jimmy Carter failed to get the point, but he didn't comment on it either.

Maintain radio silence. Roger that. Over and out.

WHY CAN'T WE SEE THE 9/11 PENTAGON SECURITY TAPES?

Some Muslim guys took a few flying lessons in single propeller airplanes and then piloted commercial airliners hundreds of miles off course on perfect flight paths into very narrow targets. This required sophisticated instrument rating navigation skills, and the ability to control altitude and turns.

One of the airplanes they hijacked was a Boeing 757, American Airlines flight 77. I'm Executive Platinum on American Airlines, so this doesn't make me happy. Executive Platinum means I fly 100,000 miles a year on that airline, which I've done for the last four years in a row. I'm not buying the story.

The Government of the United States will not release the Pentagon security tapes of Flight 77 hitting the Pentagon. Why? What legitimate reason could there be? National Security? Video footage of the grounds of the Pentagon, that anybody can drive by or walk by on the sidewalk, has to be classified for National Security reasons?

This makes absolutely no sense. Stated in mathematical terms, it makes zero sense.

What is the fake news cover story? There isn't one. The cover story is no cover story – there isn't even a fake explanation.

Notice that I'm not advancing a conspiracy theory here. I'm not saying there were aliens sitting on the wings of the airplane. I'm not saying anything except this preposterous fake news story makes no sense whatsoever. Oh, and by the way, one of the high-jackers on one of the planes that hit the twin towers was Mohammed Atta. The plane burst into flames on impact and the fire was so hot it brought the building down. However, Mohammed Atta's passport fluttered to the ground intact and was recovered there by investigators, according to the mainstream media. OK, no problem, I believe that must be what happened because it was reported in the news, for real.

BUILDING SEVEN AND THE NIST REPORT

The NIST Report, not the MIST Report. If it was the MIST Report, maybe we couldn't see things clearly. The National Institute of Standards and Technology issued the official government report on 9/11.

Imagine if I did a poll of a representative sample of the population of the United States, with only one question: "How many buildings taller than 40 stories collapsed in Manhattan on 9/11?"

I'll bet you no less than 95% of people would answer, "Two."

This would be the North Tower and the South Tower. World Trade Center One and World Trade Center Two. The twin towers. Everybody knows that. Nobody talks about the triplet towers. Two towers collapsed, everyone knows that. The initial draft of the NIST Report didn't even mention a third building.

On 9/11, two buildings were hit by airplanes. True. And two buildings taller than 40 stories collapsed. False.

What actually happened on 9/11? World Trade Center Building 7 was not hit by an airplane. Debris from 1 World Trade Center struck WTC 7, which was 47 stories tall, and started fires in the building. Burning paper and furniture in WTC 7 caused it to collapse. That's the official story. It collapsed in a perfect free fall into its own footprint.

Other than on 9/11, no skyscraper in the world built to WTC construction standards has ever collapsed from fire, despite much longer, bigger, hotter fires than those in WTC 7. The original NIST Report didn't even mention WTC 7. First, when they finally got around to talking about WTC 7, they said it was burning diesel fuel in tanks in the building that caused the collapse. Then they said 'no' to that theory and said it was office furniture and paper.

Again, I'm not advancing a conspiracy theory. I'm not saying what did happen. I'm just saying that the official story is ridiculous fake news. But you know what happened on 9/11, right? You know the facts, right? Right, Citizen Kane? You don't even know how many buildings collapsed on 9/11, but you know what happened.

Here's another news story. A UFO crashed near Roswell, New Mexico in early July, 1947. Personnel from nearby Roswell Army Air Field secured the crash scene, transported the debris back to base, and the base issued a press release announcing that a UFO had been recovered. The story was reported in the mainstream media throughout the world. Colonel William Blanchard, Commander of the 509th Bomb Group, was the officer who issued the press release.

Then, within hours of the first press release, General Roger Ramey, Commander of the Eighth Air Force at Ft. Worth Army Air Field in Ft. Worth, issued a statement that it was actually a weather balloon, not an alien spacecraft. This became the official story. Later, the weather balloon was switched to a test missile, however, Roswell researchers have proven through a study of official logs that neither a weather balloon nor a missile was launched and lost in that time period.

So here's what you have to believe in order to buy the official story, which has in any case been disproven in both of its two versions: US Army crash investigators can't tell the difference between an alien spaceship and a weather balloon. Go for it, sure, yeah, definitely, I buy that the military is that incompetent. No problem there for me. And you? As the anti-Trumpers know, only a nut like Trump would think there is fake news.

So, to reiterate, I'm not saying that an alien spaceship did crash in Roswell. What I'm pointing out is the story you are being asked to believe: a weather balloon crashed near Roswell, Army crash investigators went out and secured the scene, mistakenly thought it was a UFO, reported that to their command on the base, and as a result the base issued a press release that a UFO had crashed, then they re-examined the debris and realized it was actually a weather balloon.

VACCINE HYSTERIA AND COUNTER-HYSTERIA

The vaccine conversation in the United States is another example of a polarized intellectual gang war, with drive-by shootings in the form of ruined reputations and careers, insults, and slander as the coin of the realm. There are the pro-vaxxers and the anti-vaxxers. Both sides demonize the other and both have God on their side, or at least Science, which is the God of the pro side. For this conversation, I'm going to focus on the pro side of the coin, realizing that there are two sides to the coin.

First, everything gets reduced to two polarized options: either you are pro or anti. It is pure black and white, with no shades of grey, which is a drag for people who are into bondage. Either you are 100% for or 100% against. But let's look at reality, after the doctors have patted our heads and told us that vaccines are safe and effective.

I was taught in medical school that there are hundreds of cases of encephalopathy from the measles vaccine every year. Permanent brain damage. Even death. Why give the vaccine, then? Because it is worth it from a public health point of view to save tens of thousands of lives at the cost of killing or maiming a small number. This is true. But the pro vaxxers way, way minimize the side effects and risks. They also over-promote the effectiveness.

In the end, it doesn't make any sense to have one monolithic attitude towards vaccines. This makes no medical or scientific sense. Some vaccines are much, much more effective than others, and some of the diseases we vaccinate against are much, much more lethal and damaging than others. The cost-benefit is not the same for every vaccine. To make an informed decision, you have to evaluate the evidence in a balanced, rational, analytical manner. To do that, you need the facts. These are hard to get from the medical establishment, because they are on such a mission to stamp out anti-vaxxer hysteria that they cover up the problems with vaccines. Most doctors drink the vaccine Kool Aid daily at both breakfast and lunch.

Virtually every effective intervention in medicine kills some people. This varies from 1 in 100,000 dying from an anaphylactic reaction to a medication to 1 in 3 dying from the most high-risk surgeries. You just can't say that all medical treatments are good or all are bad. It's way more complicated than that.

But how does the vaccine conversation go in America? It's another example of the same problem, everything dumbed down to a cartoon level of simplicity, with extreme, rigid attitudes and big emotional over-reactions on both sides. Hey, I get it, those hysterical anti-vaxxers need to stop talking about MMR and autism because we took thimerosal out of the MMR vaccine a while back. Sssshhh. Don't mention that it's still in the flu vaccine. That would just feed into the hysteria, and we don't want that because then the antivaxxers might not get their kids vaccinated and our vaccinated kids might get measles despite the measles vaccine being highly effective so we don't have to worry, so let's reassure the parents that their children are safe if they get vaccinated while stirring up their fear about the danger to their kids posed by the un-vaccinated children of the anti-vaxxers. Say, pssstt – still listening? The thimerosal content of the flu vaccine is stated on the FDA website.

I'M HITTING YOU BECAUSE I LOVE YOU: AND I'M DEMONSTRATING VIOLENTLY FOR PEACE

I've spoken with many hundreds of battered women, women who've been stalked relentlessly for years by their exes, women who have been sexually abused by their fathers, uncles, and brothers, and a smaller number of women who've been abused by their lesbian partners. The overwhelming majority of perpetrators are men. They aren't really men, though, in my book, equals this book, because no man would behave like that. Only boys in men's bodies behave like that.

The batterer, psychologically, is a little boy living in a man's body. A small, scared, insecure, lost little boy who feels abandoned by his mommy. It's very scary to feel all alone and abandoned when you're only four years old. You can feel this way even when you are living with your mother, for a variety of reasons. Maybe she just isn't there emotionally, due to depression, substance abuse, her own abusive childhood, or due to being beaten down by her husband.

Now, unfortunately, that little boy lives inside a grown up body with big muscles, a big truck, a big belt buckle, a big hat and a big temper. Now mommy = the missus ain't getting' away with shit, 'cause now he's a man. He ain't gettin' abandoned no more, you can be damn sure of that. Inside every batterer is a scared little boy. But the grown up body the little boy lives in is responsible for his behavior in my book, called The Trump Card. Just because you understand his psychology, doesn't mean you have to let him get away with shit.

The grown up has to sign off on the violence, give it the green light and participate in it, if not be the prime agent of it. Despite the fact that it's an emotionally infantile choice, there is a grown up choice being made. And these guys can be incredibly relentless. The worst scenario I've heard, from a colleague, is a high-level professional who was remarried with children from his second marriage. Fifteen years after his divorce – fifteen years! – he went to a conference in another state, checked into a hotel, then went to the airport, flew across the country, rented a car, murdered his ex-wife, drove back to the airport, flew back to the convention city, and attended the rest of the conference. Fifteen years later!

The minimum sentence for this guy should be life without parole. I don't care what his childhood was like, I don't care about his mental state or his psychiatric evaluation by the defense expert. Life without parole. End of discussion. I assume that all feminists would be in agreement with this attitude. Notice that I left the death penalty out of the discussion – it's not relevant here. The point is, this guy gets the max and is held responsible for his behavior as an adult, in my book, no matter how scared a little boy there is inside. No little boy could carry out that operation.

OK. We're all on the same page then, in my book.

How many zillions of times over have battering husbands told their wives that they love them? I don't know exactly, but it's zillions.

"I just hit you because I love you so much. I'll never do it again. Don't leave me."

"I love you too," says the wife.

Three weeks later, kapow! The cycle goes on and on and on.

How many hundreds of times have I heard, "But I love him"?

The batterer's greatest weapon against his wife is her love for him. I'm sure that somewhere, in some part of himself, he does love her. But he also despises her for staying. And the crumbs of love don't count for much when you are being verbally and physically abused, cut off from friends and family, and raped on a regular basis.

This is why we have seen the burning bed defense in cases where a battered spouse kills her batterer. It's very understandable that she would feel like killing him. But in my math class, two wrongs don't make a right, unless it was self-defense with a clear and present danger, but then that's self-defense, not pre-meditated murder. Killing the guy with an axe while he's passed out on the couch is another story. Being abused as a child, or battered as a spouse, doesn't give you a license to kill, in my book.

It's very understandable that women in a chauvinistic society would be angry at men. Try being an expert on multiple personality disorder in a profession dominated by male chauvinist pigs. . . I get it. A righteous cause, in my book, is not a license to kill.

Which brings me to angry feminists threatening violence in angry marches, even, like Madonna, more or less threatening to assassinate the President of the United States. Sorry, but in my book, you have crossed over to the dark side. Being a feminist doesn't give you a license to castrate men. Freud thought that castration anxiety was caused by childhood conflicts – I think it's more likely caused by angry feminists.

I'M GREEN AND RIGHTEOUS: BUT HOW DID I GET TO THE ANTI-TRUMP DEMONSTRATION?

Speaking of demonstrations, how about them environmentalists? They picket outside the submarine base, or the nuclear power plant, or the logging operation, or wherever they pick up the scent. They're bloodhounds and they're going for the juggler. I spent four winters in the Canadian arctic, all without running water, one without electricity. In Norman Wells, I ate a lot of ptarmigan and moose meat and spent a lot of hours alone in the bush. So don't preach to me about the environment. Several of my books describe all of this – a series of books, in fact.

I'm willing to arm wrestle any white man who claims to have a deeper understanding of North American native spirituality than me, not just in his intellect, but in his body. Bring it on, bro! But how about them environmentalists! I couldn't compete with them in a self-righteousness contest. They are on God's side Big Time! Well, technically, God is on their side, since they are more holy than God, who of course is female, because a male God is just a male chauvinist power trip, whereas a female God is telling it like it is. Or no, maybe not. Maybe that's a mirror thing again.

The environmentalists are angry at the corporations and the capitalists and the men and the top 1%, that's for sure. They're not angry at Muslim men because that would be politically incorrect, even though the world champions of chauvinism and battery of women live in the Middle East. Sorry, that last sentence was a typo – please ignore it. I just didn't catch it before my book went to press. How do I know? Because that's what it says in my book.

Meanwhile, the Holy Environmentalists turned on the electric lights when they woke up in the morning, got online, ate the groceries they bought at the supermarket, drove in their cars to the demonstration, and documented the whole thing with their cell phones, then texted the proof to their friends. These environmentalists live inside the industrial machine and are completely dependent on it. They spend their daily lives fishing in a sea teeming with the material products of capitalism, and they catch and consume a lot of industrial products. You don't think Madonna is in the top 1% and living off the fruits of capitalism and big business and big entertainment?

Nothing against Madonna's career here – she is very talented, driven, focused, hard working and successful. No doubt about that. All power to her. But I'm not consenting to being bullied by her, or by her spherical object-compressing friends. Oh, by the way, who has made millions by being a sex object for men? Hmmm. . . not anybody mentioned in this paragraph.

So there you have it. That's what I see in my magic mirror on the subject of feminist environmentalists. Does this mean I'm in cahoots with the polluters of the environment? No. Why? Because I'm not in the game.

You guys are invited over to my space anytime. But you can't get in with that sanctimonious expression on your face.

By the way, do you know the name of my favorite white theologian? Sanctimonious Monk.

BATHROOMS FOR BOYS AND GIRLS

Sometimes a guy just has to take a leak. When he does, he doesn't want any girls or women anywhere near his urinal, because a man needs his space. Of course, once he's finished his business, any woman should feel free to inspect, handle, and even test drive his equipment, because he's a man, and he's ready to get it on.

Did you ever notice that all the men in erectile dysfunction TV ads are under sixty, physically fit, and hooking up with gorgeous women in their forties and fifties? Did you notice that none of these women are slutty, none are matronly, none are girlish, none have tattoos, and all are fully clothed? The advertisers have run it right down the middle – not too much like the wife, not too much like the daughter, not too much like a hooker, attractive but not slutty. You don't have to be guilty about having sex with that woman, and you're enough of a stud to get her. She wants it, and Little George can give it to her, with a little help from Big Pharma.

Men are so easy to manipulate!

Things are getting awfully confusing these days. These days, some guys just decide out of the blue that they're women, then they start cross dressing and taking hormones and next thing they're going to volunteer to get castrated. That's just not right. And it's scary because what if that could happen to me? All of a sudden a woman comes out and takes over like some alien and then where will I be?

"There's no way I'm gay," says the Macho Master of Reaction Formation.

"I ain't no woman," says the real man.

The feminine side of men should wait outside while the men are getting it done in the Men's Bathroom. Did you notice the name on the door? Men. It didn't say Girly Men. It didn't say Male Sissies. It said Men. Men, God damn it! Can't you read?

OK, the boys say to each other, we've got to come up with a strategy for all of this gender and bathroom stuff. The boys huddle up in the Men's Room (without touching each other), drink a couple of beers, get it all figured out, take a leak (without looking at each other's stuff) and are ready to make a political announcement.

The erectile dysfunction pharmaceutically corrected guys are all family men, and they care about their daughters. That's why they can't allow men dressed up like women into their daughters' restrooms. Next thing you know, pedophiles will be dressing up as trans and going into the Women's can to molest girls. This has never actually happened, but we're going to make sure it damn well never does. We're gonna make some laws, dad gummit!

How exactly are you Macho Men planning on enforcing this? Inspectors at the doors of the Women's Restroom who ask for government ID? Maybe lift up everyone's skirts for a visual confirmation that none of them have anything? Maybe a porno scanning device like TSA uses at the airport? How about a pat down?

What if trans women dressed up like men and came into the Men's Room? OMG! Next thing you know, the butch lesbians will be in there, gawkin' at our stuff. We better pass some legislation here!

Or wait a minute. Why would lesbians want to come into the Men's Room? That doesn't make any sense. Wouldn't the pedophile lesbians want to get into the Ladies Room to molest girls? They wouldn't come after boys. Oh, wait another minute. . . isn't the biggest threat to boys in the Men's Room from gay male pedophiles? They already get in all the time. OMG! They're in already? Looking at my stuff! I'm not even thinking about that.

The conversation about gender and bathrooms in America is ridiculous. The most ridiculous thing about it is the mental gyrations of the insecure males on the far right. Score one for the left on that conflict. But exactly how many options for gender are we wanting to have on census forms? I've had to go to a professional website to re-enter my gender (male) because the organization has instituted a new policy of inclusiveness. Could the left be getting a little carried away with its plurality of categories? In one organization I belong to, we now have eight categories – do we need twenty? Couldn't the census just be asking about biological gender? Is asking about biological gender automatically a human rights violation?

Could we talk about this without demonizing people who disagree with us?

WHY TRUMP AND CRUZ GOT EXPELLED FROM ELEMENTARY SCHOOL

I did some historical research. It turns out that Ted Cruz and Donald Trump went to the same private elementary school. In the gifted class at that school, which Donald got into due to donations to the school by his father, and Ted got into due his direct line with God, they had a debating class. In this debating class, Donald and Ted (he refused to be called Teddy, until he figured out that might make him sound like Teddy Roosevelt) debated each other. They both behaved exactly like they behaved later in the Republican primary debates in 2016.

Donald pulled out all the stops. He called Ted, Lyin' Ted. Lyin' Ted gave it back to Donald just as good. They insulted each other, interrupted each other, talked over each other, made lots of faces, and on and on it went. What happened?

Ted and Donald both got expelled from the school because of their behavior.

It is literally true that the behavior of politicians in America would not be tolerated in elementary school.

That's all I have to say about that.

THAT DARN BILLY BUSH!

That Billy Bush! What a character! And what a brown noser, hanging out with the Donald. Like I said, Donald's macho locker room talk is totally reaction formation. He's trying to be one of the guys. But being an insecure nerd underneath doesn't give you a license to be a male chauvinist pig.

If only Donald would learn to feel better about himself. Like him or hate him, it's a pretty amazing achievement to get elected President of the United States with no prior political experience, with a campaign that was substantially self-funded, and against the opposition of his own political party. That by itself should be grounds for all the self-esteem anyone could need. Then the business success. Hobnobbing with the rich and famous. Marrying an incredibly gorgeous model and making her the third immigrant First Lady in the history of the United States. Taking a million in seed money from your dad and turning it into a business empire.

That's quite a list of achievements. Donald, I'd really appreciate it if you would drop the "one of the guys" routine. It's unbecoming of an officer and a gentleman.

ADVANCED PSYCHOLOGICAL THEORY: OBJECT PERMANENCE

In developmental psychology, there is a concept called object permanence. If I remember right, it kicks in around 9 months. This is when the baby gets it that if he drops something off his high chair, it still exists. Kind of like when I cover my eyes, you can still see me.

Later on in child development, the child grasps the conservation of volume.

It would be nice if the political conversation in America could mature beyond concrete operations and the sensorimotor stage of development.

That's what I'm wishing for this Christmas!

EXTRODUCTION: THAT'S ALL I HAVE TO SAY ABOUT THAT

As first enunciated by that towering intellect and social commentator, Forrest Gump, that's all I have to say about that.

"Thank God, Basil. Finally we can get some sleep."

"Yes, maybe when we wake up, it will all seem like a big dream, and too crazy to be true."

And that's all folks! Not another word from me!

Word.

APPENDIX

The appendix is a vestigial organ consisting of an outpunching from the proximal ascending colon.